THE WHOLE WORLD HAS CHANGED
-*AND THE CHURCH IS ASLEEP*

A Guide to Immigrant/Diaspora Ministry

©2023 Rev. Roland J. Wells, Jr.

SDG

Version 1.0

II

Table of Contents

IV

Acknowledgments/Dedication

First, thanks to the congregation and leaders of St. Paul's Evangelical Lutheran Church for its support and vision in bringing the reality of our holistic model to reality. For over a century, the congregation's vision for training and sending young people into local and global outreach has been their passion.

Secondly, thank you to the staffs of St. Paul's, Mission*Shift* and our associated ministries for their never-ending encouragement and support over the decades this all has been developed. Special thanks to Lois Bodurtha, Patricia Lokke, Misrak Kebede Adoga, Jennifer Schewe, Andrea Scharmer, Carl and Cheryl Rich, Pr. John Spaulding, as well as our many seminary students and college interns. Thank you to Lois Bodurtha and Janet French for their proofreading and suggestions. Thank you to Jennifer Diedrick for her artistic talents.

Thirdly, thank you to all those who have served on the boards of Mission*Shift* and our associated ministries, as we have learned to teach and build. Thank you to all my co-workers in FullSpectrum, (formerly the Ethnic American Network,) and especially Dr. David Ripley for his generosity in sharing his church models. In addition, great thanks to Dr. Jeff Thormodson and the leadership at Concordia Seminary, St. Louis as they have grasped and shared our vision. Dr. Fred Hall, president emeritus of The Association of American Lutheran Churches seminary and Dr. Mark Hillmer, emeritus of Luther Seminary for their suggestions on Chapter 3. Thank you to Dr. David Ripley for allowing me to share his insights into partnership models with immigrant churches.

Fourth, I would like to thank my pastor-mentors, Rev. Dr. Morris G.C. Vaagenes, Rev. Thomas L. Basich and Rev. Irwin A. Flaten for investing themselves in me and teaching me to dream.

Fifth, I would like to thank Bill and Eva Converse, Frank and Kim Vennes, Phil and LaVerne Fandrei, Mark and Nancy Hanson, Dr. Robert and Ann Nimlos for their sacrificial gifts to make these educational programs possible.

Finally, I would like to thank my family, my wife Brenda and my sons John and Timothy, for lending their support and the many nights they have allowed me to invest in building these educational models. I also thank my parents, Roland and Pearl Wells, for teaching me to ask "Why?"

Introduction: Our Context
We Live at a Dramatic Turning Point

Today we live at the most stunning crossroad in human history. First, God is in the process of sending humanity into cities; the majority of humankind lives there now. Each of these cities is full of profound human need.

Second, we are in the midst of the greatest human migration in history. People from everywhere are moving everywhere else. The product of these two trends is the creation of global, multi-cultural megacities at a staggering rate. All of this is accelerating. This same migration is affecting every sized city and town in America, as immigrants come to seek jobs.

The global Christian Church is healthy and exploding. I saw this as a delegate to Lausanne 2010 missions gathering in Cape Town and in the Lausanne communiqués since. The Church today is brown and south. The explosion of faith in Africa, Latin America and Asia is at a rate far surpassing even the first generation of New Testament times.

Yet at the same time, the church in America and western European is imploding. Starting with the Baby Boomers, each successive generation has seen a greater and greater collapse. In the few American denominations that see growth, most of that growth is from immigrants who come here with faith.

There are many different kinds of immigrants; some win a green card through the US annual lottery, some are refugees or asylum seekers, some overstay visas or enter illegally. Each type poses special needs and offer special opportunities for ministry.

These immigrants, over two million each year, are creating a new America in our midst. These immigrants and their families perhaps number 75 million in our country. In 2014 America passed a quiet milestone: for the first time the overall number of Latino, African-American and Asian heritage students in American schools surpassed the number of non-Hispanic whites. By mid-century there will be no majority racial group in the US. Most of this change is due to immigrants and their families.

This book is neither pro- nor anti-immigration. Global migration is a fact, like air. There is probably no way to stop it. Barring some sort of world catastrophe, I can't imagine the mass-movement of people around the globe will slow down in the next few generations. American companies need cheap labor to compete with China. Many other forces, political, economic and demographic all help create the suction that is drawing millions to our land. War, famine and poverty will thrust hundreds of millions of people from their current homes. We will look at many of those factors in this book. So, what is this book about?

What is This Book About?

- Chapter One will lay out the current world situation, where globalization with its partners of urbanization and mass migration are creating a world and a mission opportunity unlike any in history.

  •Chapter Two outlines the framework for ministry we face with migrants in both urban and even rural settings, based on the process of these immigrants becoming acculturated to their new surroundings and culture. Ministry needs and locations change as a people group gets settled. Over and over again, these patterns are described by we note bell-shaped curves

  •Chapter Three is the key theological framework for ministry. How can Christians engage in social ministry without losing Gospel proclamation? Can we bring a cup of cold water *and* make disciples? The Bible contains two frameworks for God's work in the midst of humankind. These are described by the Hebrew words *mishpat* (justice) and *chesed* (covenant love). The Reformers, using Paul's terms, spoke about these frameworks as Law and Gospel. Looking at this biblical framework we are able to gain insights so we learn to do holistic Christian ministry.

  •Chapter Four considers the relationship of culture to Christianity. We say Christians are "In the world, but not of the world." What does that mean? How engaged with the surrounding culture can we be without losing our identity as Christian believers? As we face a new, unfamiliar culture to make disciples, how much of that culture needs to be rejected to be biblical believers? In America, much of the difference between fundamentalist, evangelical and mainline Christians is based not on doctrine, but in their relationship to the surrounding culture.

•Chapter Five lays out what we've learned in over thirty years about how a congregation or just a bunch of friends can study and create small, holistic ministry to reach out to a new group of immigrants in your area. This is *not* the *only* way to create a ministry, but it does serve as a model of making sure to do adequate research before creating an appropriate outreach. Most of these ministries fail, because they don't know the people who they are trying to help nor their setting.

•Chapter Six outlines methods we've developed to train people for these new tasks. Since 1995, Mission*Shift* Institute has trained over one thousand individuals to create small, flexible, contextual, cross-cultural ministries, starting with limited resources. *"Teaching Christians to Build and Lead Cross-Cultural Ministries."* I present this model to show the many competencies, areas of expertise and holistic approach we believe you need to be successful in cross-cultural diaspora ministry.

•Chapter Seven thinks through various approaches to immigrant diaspora ministry. Should our target be ethnic-specific, language-specific congregations, or multi-cultural congregations for all? When does each type work, and what can an existing congregation do to create such ministries?

•Chapter Eight presents several different models for congregations to create or assist an immigrant outreach. These are based on an outline by Dr. David Ripley of the Ethnic American Network.

•Finally, Chapter Nine gives some concrete suggestions on how you or your congregation can begin to reach out to the immigrants in your neighborhood. We can start small. Everybody has something they can give away without cost that some immigrant desperately needs. It might be how to buy a chicken, drive a car, speak English or know American terms used in the dairy industry.

Passing on those skills can be a very open channel to create relationships and bring the Gospel.

We stand at the most stark crossroad in American Church history. What will the American Church look like in 2050? In Jesus' words, *"When the Son of Man comes, will he find faith on earth?"* Luke 18:8 As the weakened American Church faces this crossroad, the key breakthrough for their future lies in opening the eyes of their members to the opportunity they face. What if we could take that "religious consumer" in the pew, and equip them quickly and inexpensively to see themselves as deeply committed "front line missionaries?" That is the purpose of this book, and all we do in our *MissionShift* education programs. Reaching our newly urbanized, multicultural world is the greatest task of the 21st Century Church. This is true in both the megacities and in the thousands of small towns where jobs have drawn immigrants, from the fruit groves of Florida, the ports of our coasts, to the dairy farms of Wisconsin, and the turkey processing plants of Minnesota.

Today, "the whole world has changed, and the church is asleep." I hope that this book will be the alarm clock to wake you, your friends, and your church to the task ahead.

-Rev. Roland J. Wells, Jr.

Chapter One: The Changing World

The whole world has changed, and the Church is asleep. The world is undergoing its greatest change in history and the Church doesn't get it, yet. Today, the world is in a "perfect storm" of change. Three factors are coming together that will have a greater impact on the history of the world than the fall of the Roman empire, the Black Death, the European settlement of the new world, everything related to WWII and even the dawning of the Nuclear Age.

This change is globalization. It is a force that will change every aspect of the way you live your life, do your job, raise your children and relate to your neighbors. It affects the foods we eat, the products we buy and how we get them. It will cause the loss and gain of personal fortunes. It must change the way the church of Jesus Christ views its ministry in every setting, from your neighborhood to the megacities of the world. Globalization is made up of three factors, which are inextricably interwoven to create a "perfect storm" of global change.

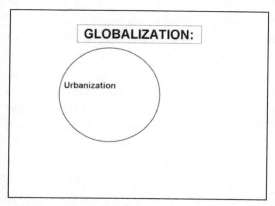

First Factor: Urbanization

The first factor is the urbanization of the world. In 1800, just three percent of the world's population lived in cities. As had been true for thousands of years, virtually all people lived in villages, small towns, family groups or in migrating clans. In 1800 there was one city of a million people in the world, London of the Industrial Revolution.

By 1900, that revolution had more than tripled the number of people who lived in cities, ten percent. After World War II, the graph went vertical. By 2000, fifty percent of the world's six billion people lived in vast, multicultural cities. Most amazingly, at that rate, by *2050 seventy-five percent of the world's people will live in cities.*[i]

Moreover, all around the globe, rural areas are emptying out. The World Mission Prayer League is a global mission agency our congregation has worked with for decades. They have had missionaries serving in Andean villages in Ecuador for seventy-five years. Today churches there are closing, because the population is plummeting; young folks are moving to the cities. Recently 1,000 people a week left Ecuador, mostly for Spain and the

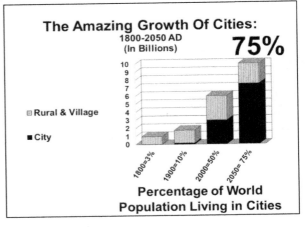

United States. In western Montana, entire towns are disappearing. Large counties now have two or three high schools; farmers commute a few times a year to plant, tend and harvest their tens of thousands of acres of wheat. In 2000, three billion people lived in small towns and rural areas. By 2050, that will shrink to two and a half billion.

These new cities are exploding all over the globe, but particularly in Asia. Even by the late 1990s, UN population maps show the pattern of the future. Beyond that, the large cities of South American, Africa, south Asia and even Europe continue to expand. Cities in the majority world are often surrounded by vast slums with extremely low employment and indescribable conditions of hygiene and sanitation. The UN terms cities of ten million "megacities." In 1950 there was one megacity, New York. By 1985 that number had grown to nine. In 2004 it was 19. 2009 it was 30; by 2015 it passed 60! Have you heard of Shenzhen or Tianjin? Both Chinese cities have over ten million people! A few years ago, my wife experienced a three-week tour of China. Driving across these vast metropolises, as far as the eye can see, in every direction there are clusters of 25- to 40-story housing towers being built at a dizzying rate. God is sending 75 percent of humanity into vast, challenging, multicultural cities by 2050.

Second Factor: Migration

As the cities grow, they are growing with people from all over the world. In 1974, the Lausanne Congress on International Evangelization set the agenda for world missions for the end of the Twentieth Century. The task was simple:

1. Go deeper and deeper into rural areas to find every "people group."
2. Coordinate outreach to these "unreached people groups" so that ten mission organizations wouldn't send missionaries to one group, and none to the other nine. The focus was on going further up the rivers and deeper into the jungles and mountain ranges to find and reach each of these people groups.

What missiologists did not guess in 1974 was that twenty years in the future, people anywhere could somehow afford passage to anywhere else. *People from everywhere are moving everywhere else.* Today, the unreached people groups might be the diaspora of Bulgarians in Berlin, or Chinese in Bogota. There are Somalis in Sweden, Chinese in Chile, Tajiks in Toledo and over 100 languages, perhaps 150 distinct people groups in south Minneapolis! Some estimate that two billion people are on the move across the globe, within their own countries, or crossing borders. The Chinese government, in just one program is moving 420 million landless peasants into cities.

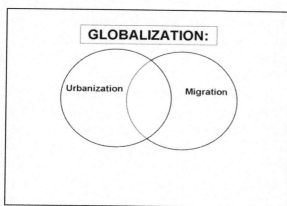

A few years ago, a missionary with 30 years of experience in Kenya told me about large communities from Pakistan, India, China and even South America who have come to Nairobi to settle and do business. In Minneapolis, I have met Swedish Somalis and Australian Somalis, settled in those countries as refugees by the UN, who have moved in a secondary migration on tourist visas to Minneapolis. Missional diaspora demographer John Mayer of CityVision believes that Minneapolis' Phillips neighborhood may be the one single most diverse in the nation. Minnesota's long history of refugee resettlement, beginning after World War II, has given the Twin Cities an amazing diversity, with four times as many UN refugees per capita as any metro area in the United States.   Along with this is a huge increase of documented and undocumented immigrants.   Fifteen years ago, one in eleven people in our three million metro area was a new immigrant. Today it is nearing one in four: nearly a million immigrants in our metro area of four million.   Using US Census data, information from real estate websites and talking to your local school officials, you can discover the background of the thousands of immigrants surrounding you.

The United States allows one million new immigrants into the country each year by means of its "lottery." Millions of people all over the world apply to the United States with hope of gaining one of those slots. Beyond this, more than a million people come to the United States without documentation. Some come on tourist visas and disappear.   More than a million come here by crossing our borders illegally. Entire American industries, such as construction, meatpacking, hotels and restaurants could not function without these immigrants.   America's low birth rate for the past 50 years has created a shortage of workers.   In another chapter, we will see that more are on the way.

America is uncertain about what to do with this influx. State and local governments are most concerned with the rising costs of medical care and educational costs for these immigrants.   Meanwhile, the Federal government is paralyzed with the issue, in part because 12 million undocumented immigrants are pumping perhaps $50 billion into the Social Security Trust Funds on false Social Security numbers annually. This is money those immigrants can never reclaim, and it is providing perhaps one sixth of the fund's annual income!

All over the globe, this intra- and international migration diaspora is creating challenges.   Most of these huge cities have virtually no treatment of sewage and poor treatment of drinking water. These growing cities not only produce human waste, they also produce industrial waste.   The level of heavy metals and other dangerous industrial toxins in Chinese waters is almost unthinkable, and it is getting worse.   About two percent of Chinese sewage receives wastewater treatment; the rest goes directly into rivers. When traveling in Ecuador, people there told me that the sewage from their city of a quarter million people goes untreated directly into the local river, where it becomes the drinking water for the next city downstream.

In every exploding city, there exists the same needs of clean water, education, health care, economic development and support of the family. With all this change and turmoil, the family is the greatest place of need. For thousands of years, young marriages were held together by their families. Young couples were encouraged, cajoled, scolded, listened to, mentored and sometimes shamed by parents, aunts, uncles, grandparents, in-laws. Young marriages have many challenges, and without a village and its corresponding taboos, wisdom, responsibilities and love, many fail. It doesn't take a village to raise a child, it takes a marriage to raise a child, but it takes a village to hold that young marriage together. Wherever urbanization happens, along with it comes a rise in divorce as those isolated marriages come apart; the nuclear family explodes. On the way there, the relationships are often filled with abuse and violence. Urban settings create and intensify great human need.

In most parts of the world, there is no welfare safety net, and soon women and children are destitute. In Tijuana, Mexico, a handful of miles from the U.S. border, we visited the local dump with a local ministry a few years ago. Thousands of women and children waited in the city dump, destitute and scrounging, waiting for their husbands or boyfriends to return. Southern California ministries went weekly to this site to bring food and clothing. Poverty was so acute that a squabble might break out over a single dropped bean. Divorce often leads to prostitution, HIV and orphans. South American cities are filled with homeless children, called "shoeshine boys."

My son served for several months on a Youth With a Mission (YWAM) team in Colombia. On my desk, I have a picture he took of two little girls who are such orphans. I would've loved to include it, but it's impossible to get permission to use their image. One was age four and the other 18 months. On the day he took the picture, the girls had come to the mission to receive baths and clean clothes. They got some new barrettes for their hair, and even had a bit of fun with face painting; but then I look into their eyes. The older one's eyes are full of pain and distrust. The younger... it looks like there's nobody home. At 18 months, she has already checked out. In these communities of kids, the older children give some care to these little ones, but not much. They support themselves by constantly pilfering. They sleep in "puppy piles" to keep warm. They also support themselves by prostitution. The day the picture was taken, the younger girl was being treated for gonorrhea.

We can talk about a billion here and a million there- but finally, we come down to individuals like these children.   As these vast global megacities grow, there is cost in human lives.

Third Factor: Fluidity of Capitol, Labor and Information

In the last month, someone on a telephone help line has probably assisted you, who was on the other side of the globe.   Whether it was settling an insurance claim, ordering from a website or arranging your vacation, you probably spoke to someone in India, Indonesia or even Ireland.   A friend of mine who specializes in computer networking for a large health services provider oversees three large call centers in India. One of our congregation's members has a small software firm.   He served as a missionary to India in the 1970s and fell in love with the people and cultures.   His office is in the United States' Midwest.   His programmers are all in Bangalore.

Mold makers, highly specialized machinists, have been one of the most stable skilled blue-collar professions in America.   As you look at the pen beside you, or your mobile phone case, each piece of plastic came from a mold, which was skillfully carved by machinists.   These molds are very expensive and carefully crafted.   Until recently, these jobs were seen as irreplaceable in America.   Today, a plastics firm can email a blueprint to a Chinese firm who will make the mold in one-third the time and for one-fourth the cost.   Their workers work in three shifts each day, and the mold is simply Fed-Exed to the American firm.

Today more people speak English in China than in America.   In an instant, people anywhere on the globe can communicate ideas via the Internet.   Telephone communications have become so inexpensive that transglobal phone calls are the norm for billions of people.   Somali refugees have told me of old copies of the Minneapolis phone book being available in Somali refugee camps in Kenya, helping soon-to-be relocated

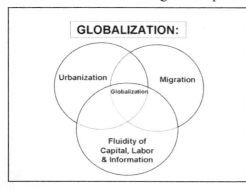

Somalis arrange their new lives. How communications have changed!   In 1974, I toured Europe with the University of Minnesota Concert Band Ensemble.   From Salzburg, Austria, I phoned home for three minutes at a cost of about $125 in today's money.   Now I could make that same call for less than a quarter!

A recent Public Radio story told of a Taiwanese firm that was closing its plants in Laos and moving them to Cambodia because labor and environmental laws were more lenient there. Thomas Friedman's book, *The World Is Flat: A Brief History of the Twenty-first Century*[2] became a best-seller because it clearly demonstrates the tremendously fluid nature of labor, capital and information. Global markets influence all competition for jobs, sources of labor and the location of manufacturing. Workers may work at home for companies fifteen time zones away. Catastrophes, weather phenomena and market forces on the other side of the globe may strengthen or destroy a local company. The prices an Indiana farmer receives for soybeans may be determined by a drought in Brazil or flooding in China. Today American firms manufacture all over the globe, while China is buying American iron mines. The interlocking of multinational corporations, capital and the availability of labor interplays with the vast migration of humanity and rapid urbanization. The world of 2050 will be immensely different from today in how manufacturing, sales, communication and every other aspect of commerce will be done.

A Holistic Model

As we look at these tremendous needs, we can also see them as tremendous opportunities for reaching people in the Name of Jesus. We see that this task has three components:

1) Proclamation of the Gospel is the central task of the Christian Church. The Gospel is the message that Jesus Christ took on himself the sins of the world so that humanity can be reunited with God. By trusting in Christ,

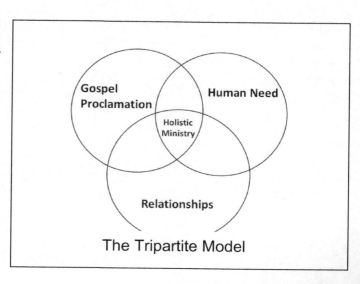

The Tripartite Model

we are forgiven of our sins and made to be one with God. That is the Gospel; Paul said that there was no other. Paul also says that faith comes from hearing that message, "Faith comes by hearing, and hearing by the preaching of Christ." (Romans 10:17) That is the central purpose of the Church, and faith in Christ is the greatest gift we can give to all people, but that proclamation does not exist in a vacuum.

2) **Vast Human Needs** are a part of every global city. Virtually all human needs are created by some lack of justice. Part of God's work in his world is to create and sustain order and justice. These are needs that must be met, but how do we do that without creating even more dependency? There will be more on that in chapter four. The bottom line is that each of these needs is a channel for the Gospel.

3) **Relationships** are the key to each of these, as both the Gospel and care are most effectively transmitted when we take the time to build healthy, culturally-savvy relationships.

The Yoiddo Full-Gospel Church in Seoul, Korea has learned how these circles interlock. They have built a church of *800,000* members by teaching its members to simply look for hurting people and love them into the Kingdom of God. This congregation is built entirely of cell groups, called "house churches." Each house church covenants to bring into their group a certain number of new believers each year. They simply look for hurting people, surround them with love, take care of the needs, and disciple the new believer. In their church's teaching, they term this need, "divine desperation," believing that God is in the midst of bringing this new believer to faith through these very needs! Each human need is a channel for relationship building and proclamation of the Gospel.

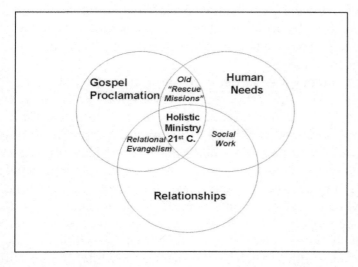

If we take any two of the circles together, we see a popular ministry model. If we only have Gospel proclamation and human need, we have the model of the old-line rescue mission- "soup, sermon, soap and sleep." The Gospel was faithfully proclaimed and human needs met; but the long-term discipling relationship that brought real change was often missing. If we have Gospel proclamation and relationship, then we have friendship evangelism. That's great, but in the megacities it is not enough. If we have human need and relationship, we have good social work. There is nothing wrong with that, but if we combine all three, we have the model of Jesus, of Paul, of Wesley, Spener, Hauge and Hudson Taylor, to name a few. The model has been rediscovered repeatedly throughout the history of the Church.

"Old Urban" Versus "Glocal"

With all these global factors, we can see that we are approaching a new era in urban/cross-cultural ministry. A later chapter will develop this theme more fully. As an introduction, from the 1960s to the 1980s, the American church saw the development of a standard model of urban ministry.

It was based on the social optimism of the New

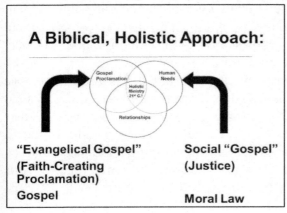

Deal of Roosevelt and the Great Society of Johnson. It was highly informed by the "social gospel" which hit its peak in the mid-20th century, although later it readily absorbed the themes of Liberation Theology. These great leaders began to awaken the Church, but they faced an urban world very different from today.

The "old urban" model was partially driven in the '50s and '60s by thousands of young men who were social progressive, Vietnam War pacifists, those who received the "divinity deferments[3]" from the draft. This skewing of the politics of the clergy of the mainline churches left a permanent mark on the American church scene. Many of these progressive students were interested in issues such as poverty and racial justice and thus felt drawn to the core city. Much of the emphasis of the old urban ministry model stressed intervention in social and political issues. It faced endemic poverty and dealt with relationships between cultures that were well known to each other, and in fact, like siblings grew up in opposition to each other, such as the black and white divide. In chapter four we are going to review and critique this model, offering a new and very old model for doing social ministry without losing Gospel proclamation.

The holistic model that is forming now sees the healing of the 20th Century American divide between the "social gospel" and the "evangelical gospel." (There is one Gospel; the "social gospel" is about justice and the Law; we will work on that one in chapter three.) The person of Jesus Christ is the only one who can unify our culture and bring hope and wholeness to people. The holistic gospel approach meets human needs and is boldly evangelical. It deals with poverty, but many of the new international arrivals are quite upwardly mobile, quick to migrate within an urban center and often finding great prosperity.

The cross-cultural and social challenges of the city are now evident in every suburb, small city and town. All local ministry now has a global content, and all global ministry comes down to the neighborhood. Hence, in the 21st Century, all effective ministry will have to be "glocal." Politically this new movement is undefined, but it has room for those across the spectrum. Most notably, the "new urban" glocal ministry is to and with people whose cultures have little history together, neither positive nor negative, and certainly, the cultures have not had time to define themselves over against each other, developing hardened walls.

For example, in the upper Midwest, there is little prejudice towards Hispanic people. Historically there has been little contact with Latinos, and in many places, their presence is welcomed with ample employment and enjoyment of their cultural uniqueness. Comparing this to long-term interaction and tension in the Southwest, the difference is striking. At the same time, Midwestern Hispanics are far from fully integrated into every aspect of society. They are still very much outsiders and even curiosities to many in the rural areas they are now entering for work.

"Glocal" ministry is not limited to the core city. New diaspora immigrants are part of the double whammy of urbanization and globalization that focuses this "new urban" ministry not only at the core city, but even in fifth ring suburbs, small towns and rural areas. This new type of cross-cultural ministry needs a better name- not urban, but "glocal" or "diaspora" ministry. This will be the challenge of the American and global Church for the first half of the 21st Century. To reach our new neighbors, we need to change the self-understanding of every member of the pew from religious consumers to front-line missionary! Every church in America needs to train its members to do simple cross-cultural holistic missions.

Entrepreneurial Ministry is the Key

I began ministry in small town Minnesota. When I lived in these rural areas, I collected the histories of the area's congregations, founded right after the Civil War. Those immigrant pastors were imaginative, passionate, gutsy, half-crazy circuit riders who often preached at three or four preaching points a Sunday. They rode horseback through a country that less than a decade before had seen bloody warfare between settlers and Native Americans who had seen too many promises broken. These pastors oversaw the building of churches as logs were cleared from the land. They were paid in hay, firewood or potatoes, and built a lively, pragmatic piety that has never been snuffed out.

Today, ministry to our new diaspora neighbors needs that same entrepreneurial spirit. Bold immigrant pastors work long hours after working full-time in jobs to feed their families. They build strong, holistic-thinking congregations, marked by cultural hallmarks that often show a very different understanding of the same Bible used by established churches. These churches boldly build congregations, minister to their people and serve as family away from home. They grieve and puzzle over young people who straddle two cultures, children who have a hard time remaining in their language-specific congregation as they grow older.

These churches are fiercely independent, isolated and often fail or split. They mirror the same denominational differences as other American churches, plus they often have hidden cultural divides, which are hard for outsiders to understand. For example, very few churches for ex-Hindus exist in the United States. Even though East Indians may share a language, traditional caste differences can make egalitarian relationships in an Indian church too uncomfortable for them to overcome. Northern Mexicans see themselves as being very different from those of the south or even those from around Mexico City. These differences can be hard to overcome, even in the church.

In chapters seven and eight of this book we will explore opportunities, methods, models and cultural considerations for partnering with such entrepreneurial ministry start-ups for immigrants. Immigrants follow predictable patterns of entering their new culture and becoming acculturated. In chapter two we will consider these patterns of acculturation and their significance in creating and finding proper locations for such ministries.

The Challenge of Right Now

The existing church has a particular opportunity in our generation. Our society faces an uncertain future. What sort of combined identity will we have as a nation? Will we be *E pluribus unum,* one from many? In many parts of our world, cultures have remained distinct and conflict-prone for centuries.

Our congregation has had over 100 seminary students pass through it in the past 30 years. One of our congregation's former seminarians illustrates this strikingly, a second-career pastor. He had grown up as a child in what became East Germany. His family were large landowners, and as the Russians came through at the end of the war, his family fled to Argentina, where he spent his teen years as a *gaucho* cowboy on the vast *pampas*. He next went to Montana for college, where he met an American girl and settled down.

In his fifties, Jesus Christ broke into his life and he sensed a call to seminary. Upon graduation, the Lutheran World Federation approached this tri-lingual pastor to do ministry in...Romania! It turns out that Romania has a large German population who settled there a while back. They live in their own culture. They speak a German dialect they call "Saxone," which is incomprehensible to modern German speakers. They have huge "castle churches" in which to hide when the community is threatened. As a hint, at the Reformation, they decided to be Lutheran. They have existed alongside those of Romanian and Roma cultures. They have not intermarried; they have carried on their worship in High German. *Moreover, they have kept a separate culture for over 800 years!*

The cultures America brought together in the "melting pot" were closely related, mostly from northeastern Europe. Even Norwegians and Greeks share a very large part of their culture and worldview. They both have a basic understanding of Christianity. They share a common sense of Western Law. They share a common sense of what reality is, and even speak related Indo-European languages. They share the same Bible, even if they have a very different history. As close as they are, they have not joined the same churches. Even Norwegians and Swedes have had a hard time coming together in a city or church.

Compared to Norwegians and Greeks, which probably share 90 percent of their culture, let's consider a group such as Somalis. Students of our Mission*Shift* Institute reported that over 90 percent of Somalis lived as wandering pastoralists in their home country, like Sarah and Abraham! They have lived in a very concrete, clan-based society. They had no written language until the 1970s. Their understandings of duty, the roles of women and men, family, honor, time, possessions, rights, and just about every aspect of their worldview is radically different from their American neighbors.

How will American society be one? From where will we gain our identity? The purpose of this book, of our educational programs and of "glocal" model is to find unity in Jesus Christ. I believe he is the greatest hope for our country and our dizzily changing world. Will we be like the "melting pot" of the 20th Century, or the hardened cultural islands of Romania mentioned above?

This book will look at several areas of challenge and seek to open up the eyes of a new generation to its greatest challenge. The challenge of bringing Jesus Christ to this new world will be in the context of a rapidly urbanizing world, filled with young people, one filled with desperate needs, in the midst of incredible change, in cities with profound needs for food, hygiene, water, education and order. The next 100 years will be filled with conflict in a world that struggles for access to energy, resources, food and capital. It is filled with conflict as peoples long-separated suddenly collide in a rapidly shrinking world. Again, I believe that the person of Jesus Christ is our greatest hope.

For the past century, the birthrate of the United States has had an oscillating pattern. After WWI, there was a baby boom until the crash of 1929. The birth rate remained lower during the Great Depression and WWII. After the war, the Baby Boomers were born from 1945-'64. Then the children of the depression gave birth to a smaller generation, Gen X, 1964-'80. When the small Generation X entered the workforce in the 1990s, at the peak of the retirement of the large WWII generation, we had a labor shortage. That triggered the first large wave of illegal immigration.

The Baby Boomers gave birth to the Millennials 1980-'95. Here's the key: As Gen Z, the children of Gen X, enter the labor force around 2020, it will be at the peak of the Baby Boomers' retirement. We will have a labor shortage, again. *In the next decade or so, we will see another huge wave of immigration into the United States.* This book is about reaching our neighbors and getting ready for that wave. And the next.

Chapter Two:
Three Bell-Shaped Curves and How They Describe the Acculturation Process
Introduction:

Omar is a new Somali immigrant. When he comes to the United States, a social service organization settles him in inexpensive rental housing in a core-city neighborhood. In the first weeks, he is surrounded by the chaotic images of American culture. He is overwhelmed by the newness— things like light switches, finding food, bus schedules, communication with his child's school, handling of funds and thousands of other facts of American life, which were strange, felt wrong and needing to be mastered. His culture shock is powerful and unsettling.

Gradually, Omar begins to learn the system of life in Minneapolis. He learns about snow. He is welcomed by an evangelical ministry, which helps him learn the basics for ninety days. They begin to teach him about life here. He learns about banks, laws, geography, language, work readiness and many other things in the first few months. Soon he is able to get a job, buy a car, and finally move out of the chaotic city core to a more stable ethnoburb where more Somalis are settling, building stores, social services and other things that lend a sense of normalcy.

He learns rules about child abuse and how that affects disciplining his children. His wife confronts him with new roles for women. He is puzzled, amazed and revolted as he learns about American families by watching *The Simpsons, Modern Family* and *The Waltons*. He begins to learn the confusing, complicated and self-contradicting American culture. Within a few years, life has developed a new sense of normalcy and settledness. He has reached the point of being about as acculturated as he will become. He may or may not ever wish to become assimilated into what he perceives as the broader American culture; in fact, many new immigrants may strongly wish not to be assimilated, but they will become acculturated enough to function here.

Omar is a part of a people group that came to a new land. He is neither an early nor a late arriver. Others had blazed the path he followed. Later he will bring his parents and a brother to the United States, a common pattern. Finally, Omar may never become fluent in English, but he will be about average in his level of adjustment to the new culture. In a few years, he will enjoy English language television and movies. He will easily shop in stores. He will always use a translator to deal with important matters, like school and hospital, but he will be able to feel a part of the community in which he lives.

Contrasting with Omar is Habib. Habib is one of the first Somalis who came here at the beginning of our current Somali wave of immigration. He is a Somali with a degree from an Italian university, including some English. When I first worked with him, it was easier to communicate in my Spanish-laden Italian than in English. He arrived early, learned the acculturation process and mastered the social service system. He developed good work skills, good English, and today is involved in community organizations. He now makes a good income by serving the Somali community. English has become a strong fifth language, and he hopes someday to serve in city government.

Simply put, as people come to our country and learn to function, we can see some predictable patterns as they reach the *level of ability to function in this culture* they wish to reach. This is called acculturation. Each of these immigrants' experience of acculturation can be charted on each of three separate bell-shaped curves, which universally describe the acculturation process for new international immigrants. In this chapter, I'll describe from my observations, these three bell-shaped curves that illustrate this process and their implications for ministry.

Why is this important to the church? If we understand the shape and process of acculturation, we can better target evangelical and social ministry to people according to their point in the acculturation process. We can find better locations for ministries to reach these target populations. We can better focus ministries to reach changing populations, and we can better understand how to do ministry most effectively, as God sends about two million new immigrants to the United States yearly. By 2050 there will be no single majority racial group in America. Our country is changing very, very quickly. Will the church of Jesus Christ wake up to the opportunity before us?

Bell-Shaped Curves

Statistics, anthropology and sociology make constant use of the bell-shaped curve. Most human and natural phenomenon seem to fall in a natural distribution on this curve. Whenever we graph the measurements of a population, such as IQ, body weight, or hours worked per week, the results will form a bell-shaped curve. For example, a few adults weigh 75 pounds; a few weigh 750 pounds; most fall closer to an average. As I have dealt with immigrants over the past three decades, I've observed that the acculturation process follows this type of curve in several ways.

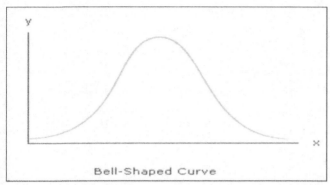

Bell-Shaped Curve

1. Group Acculturation Curve

Immigrants come to another country because of a need. Often people leave their country because they have to. War, famine, political upheaval or even genocide create a situation where people are displaced and need relocation. Often these people had no desire to leave their homes. Some emigrate with families intact. Some come as individuals or family fragments. Some have experienced horrible trauma, torture or have witnessed family members being killed. Most UN sponsored refugees are here because they have no other option.

Other immigrants come here with different needs. Many come seeking opportunity and financial gain. Some of them plan to return home. Others come here to earn money and gain citizenship for their unborn children. Most come because they do not have such opportunity at home. In time, that situation may change as their homeland becomes more prosperous. Today we see very few western Europeans, Koreans or Japanese emigrating; they have no need to leave home to find opportunity.

Each immigrant group's migration will last a finite number of years. In most UN refugee situations, this migration is event-related, such as in the aftermath of a war or famine. These migrations will last five to ten years, as camps are created. Most refugees will return to their own country or live in permanent camps in their country of exile. Only about one percent are relocated to a third country. Gradually the refugee-creating crisis ends, their living

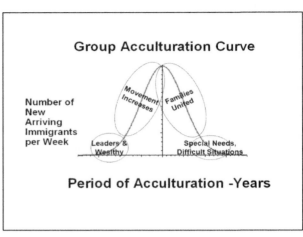

situation reaches some point of equilibrium, a few refugees are resettled in a third country, and the wave of immigrants to America from that group ends.

Other migrations, such as that of Mexican people to jobs in the United States, may be a process of one or two generations. When the American economy booms, the number of Americans available to enter the workforce shrinks, then there is a greater need for workers and the tide of immigrants increases. That wave will last until immigration becomes too difficult or there is not enough financial incentive to leave family and friends behind. In the years following the 2008 real estate meltdown, millions of Mexicans returned home with their American-citizen children. Many of those children may rightfully return to the US in adulthood.

Will the influx of Mexican people continue? When we look at the phenomenal economic growth of post-war Japan, then Korea and Taiwan, we can see that many countries can make a transformation to a modern, thriving economy in a generation. For our time, the emigration of Hispanic peoples seems a given; we will probably see increased immigration in the upcoming years, but that could end as conditions in Mexico or the US change.

Immigration Patterns Caused by Our Population Undulations [9]

To see the pattern of American immigration, we need to look at the chart of US births in the 20th Century.

As we can see in the graph, after WWI there was a little baby boom, which tapered off in the '20s and remained low through WWII. After the war, the Baby Boomer generation exploded on the scene. By the mid-sixties, that generation had quit having children and the smaller Depression generation started having children, "Generation X." This group was smaller: women began working outside of the home more, the Pill was invented, economic doldrums set in after the 1973 oil crisis, and simultaneously we began to abort one-third of our children. This is the background of the much smaller Generation X.

About 1980 we saw a new spike: the Baby Boomers began to have children, the Millennials. In the mid-nineties, we see another, smaller downtick as Gen X began to have babies. We'll call them "Generation Z." This is another small cohort, who will be reaching the labor market just before 2020.

The small Gen X cohort hit the labor market in the nineties, at the peak of the retirement of the WWII generation, at a time of a booming economy. That created the first large wave of illegal immigration in the late 1980s. We simply did not have enough workers. Here is the bottom line: as we move through the 2020s, we will see that same pattern. We will simultaneously hit the peak of Baby Boomer retirement as the small Gen Z enters the labor force. We will once again see another large wave of immigration. *Will the Church wake up?*

Some mitigating factors will affect the size of this immigration bubble. Many Baby Boomers have saved little for retirement and may not fully retire. Many Latino children, born in the US to undocumented parents, have returned to their home countries, but plan return to the US to claim their birthright US citizenship in the 2020s. They will have excellent English and job skills, having been raised part of their life in the US. They will return here with a foot in each culture, with the same legal ability to enter the US for work, like any other US citizen. The number of workers needed will depend on how robust the US economy is. Finally, adding alien workers may be encouraged by our government, perhaps with some sort of entrance surcharge or immigrant tax. They will be sorely needed to sustain Social Security and pay down the huge US national debt.

Group Immigration Patterns

As we look at the first curve, "Group Acculturation," the left tail of the

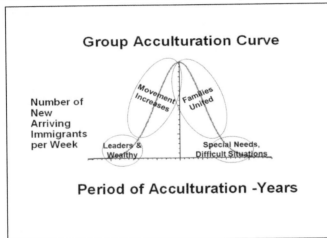

curve describes the early arrivers. This small group are those who are able to leave their troubled home early. Often, they are educated, powerful people and leave with substantial funds. Some of the early arrivals in our city have included former ambassadors, professionals, military leaders, the ruling elite and the wealthy. They have gotten out of their country "when the gettin' was good." They often left with substantial resources. They understand leadership and power, positioning themselves in the new land as those who will benefit from the one who come later. These leaders help create the programs to receive the following, larger group of refugees.

When that flow begins, local social service agencies gear up to meet them. Those who come next have many needs. They begin to get settled, aided by the early arrivals. At some point the migration hits its peak, then those here bring over their families, the refugee camps are cleared out, and the migration dwindles down. Often those at the right end of the curve are more elderly, have more physical needs or need other special care. This takes special ministry planning.

For example, since the end of the Vietnam War, there have been five distinct waves of Hmong immigration. (Hmong are a people group who lived in the mountains of Laos and worked with the CIA in the hidden war in Laos.) Later waves were smaller than the first. The later waves were caused as the various surrounding countries closed camps and forced the expulsion of refugees. The smaller migrations took less time, and were smaller, narrower curves; the pattern was the same. The Somali emigration from camps in Kenya followed this pattern but was clipped in mid-curve by the events of 9/11. A second, smaller bump has followed as carefully screened individuals and family members of earlier arrivals have been allowed to enter the US.

Building Simple Ministries to Fit the Curve

As these cohorts enter the US, there are many ramifications for ministry. As the Christian church first learns that a group is coming, it is *then*, before the group even enters our country, which is a time for immediate study of the people, its culture, its history and its needs. Churches who desire to reach immigrant populations would do well to watch for each coming wave. It is a time for savvy churches to get in contact with social service providers and learn as much as possible about the new group, and as much as the social agencies allow, to work with them to develop strategies for the church to do holistic outreach and proclamation. As we move into this new world of intense immigration, *every* congregation in America needs a cross-cultural ministry team, just as it has a Sunday School or women's group. It doesn't need to cost a lot, and a pastor doesn't need to lead it. As the members are trained with simple tools to come alongside immigrants, it changes the "religious consumer" in the pew to a new identity: that of front-line missionary. Today every congregation and every believer are now called to world missions in their midst. Global is local; local is global: "glocal."

One our key insights has been, *"Everybody has something they can give away without cost, to somebody else who desperately needs it."* Each immigrant group, at each stage has particular needs. Where we can match their needs to our ability to give them something we can freely give, that is God's prepared "access point." We can come alongside these immigrants, with simple ministries to help with the need they are experiencing at that point of their acculturation process. Without cost except our time, we can teach people how to shop in a grocery store, how to clean an apartment, how to walk on ice, give driving lessons, teach ESL, or help with citizenship classes. Through these actions, we can create relationships and introduce our new friends to Jesus. It doesn't take lots of organization, money or time. It doesn't take a ministry; all it takes is *you*. It simply takes a little creativity, an eye watching for opportunities, and a loving heart. These ministries don't have to last forever, and won't, because that group will move on. So now let's look at these curves and see how they can teach us to do appropriate ministry.

As the wave begins, identifying the future leaders and building relationships with them is critical. If these leaders can be befriended and

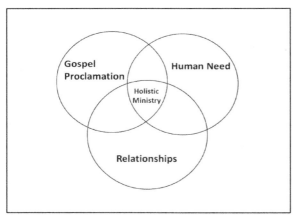

brought to faith, it will have a huge impact on the community. *Building relationships through service* is a critical opening point, and anywhere else along their acculturation journey. These immigrants will never forget those who helped them in their hour of need. As I've said before, we believe that the Biblical model can be pictured as three overlapping circles—*Proclamation of the Gospel, Meeting Human Needs and Building Relationships.* Where those three intersect, we will find the model of Jesus, Paul, Spener, Francke, Wesley and many others: *holistic ministry.*

As the immigrant group continues to grow, continued relationship building via attention to their needs will offer many channels for the Gospel. The welcoming of family members and the building of family ministries becomes possible. Evangelistic ministry for seniors of these groups is almost unheard of. Giving space and support for gatherings of elderly international immigrants is compassionate and can open doors. This new ministry to tens of millions of immigrants will take creativity. We don't want to fulfill the saying: *"Where there is no vision, it's an American parish."*

2. Individual Experiential Acculturation Curve

As these individuals come to their new land, we can describe their individual experience by a second curve. As immigrants enter the country, they are overwhelmed. At first, culture shock creates depression and resistance; then they slowly begin to learn. As the person begins to explore their new situation, they begin to learn things like:
-food acquisition
-how to live in an American apartment
-cooking food
-handling money
-customs
-geography
-gender roles
-language
-signage
-driving
-how commerce works
-communication tools
-work skills
-social service resources
-child rearing/abuse rules
-And a thousand other things.

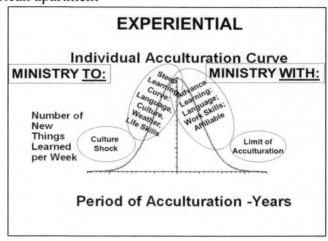

After the initial culture shock, they enter a second phase. The learning curve becomes steep and the amount of new information learned weekly is immense. As time goes on, the person gets more settled and that's when they go over the top of the curve. They probably get advanced training but need to learn less and less as time goes on. Life orders itself into a new set of default norms and the immigrant becomes as acculturated/assimilated as they will become. This may take five years, a decade, or more.

As immigrants follow this curve, they will go through many changes. At first, they will probably live in a poor-quality apartment in the core city where public transportation is available. They will need to learn basic life skills and some English. They are moving from outsider to insider in terms of culture.

Moving Forward on the Curve

As time goes on, they will gain work skills, get jobs, move to a safer place and build their new sense of identity. They will learn to feel more comfortable in their new surroundings. They may move to an area where there are more people who share their ethnicity; many cities worldwide are discovering growing "ethnoburbs" in their midst, as groups spontaneously find common areas for community. In many American cities the number of immigrants has become so large that the ethnoburbs now make up first, second and even third ring suburbs. As the Baby Boomers inherited their parents' homes, they have sold or rented them to immigrants. These are still very nice places to live; there will be few visible changes. You will see stores and businesses with signs in other languages. School kids will come in many skin tones. Yards may be decorated and landscaped in ways that look different. You may see a few extra cars in the driveway. The schools and real estate agents will be very aware of these changes and will become your key advisors on changing trends.

Ministry to people on the left side of the curve will be focused on welcoming. These people have many needs, are suffering culture shock, and will have a hard time getting beyond their needs and expand themselves into relationships. The people on the left side of the curve are people you will "do ministry *to*" rather than "do ministry *with*." They have little ability to join a congregation or get beyond their basic needs. They are focused on survival, not relationships. For these people, simple ministries explaining, "how things work here" are key. These folks may need supportive ministry for spouse abuse, school liaison, etc. They need someone to listen and come alongside them. They need clothing, food, furniture and other basic items. Each of these are ways to build relationships and bring the Gospel. They need culturally-savvy friends who speak their language, but a beginning friendship doesn't require shared language.

Location, Location, Location

These "welcome ministries" will often be sited in the core city or wherever social service providers make housing available. As the number

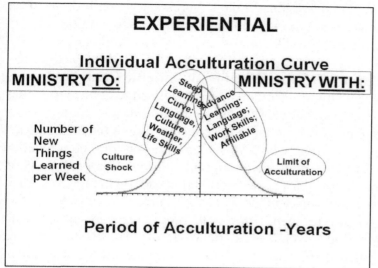

EXPERIENTIAL

Individual Acculturation Curve

MINISTRY **TO:** MINISTRY **WITH:**

Number of New Things Learned per Week

Culture Shock

Steep Learning Curve: Language, Culture, Weather, Life Skills

Advance Learning: Language; Work Skills; Affiliable

Limit of Acculturation

Period of Acculturation -Years

of immigrants increases, many times large clusters of immigrants will appear in suburban or even rural environments, due to the availability of affordable housing or entry level jobs. These locations need

to be learned and such ministries located in very close proximity. It may well be that these ministries will begin with one ethnic group and morph to another as the first wave moves on and a second takes its place. Our core-city Minneapolis neighborhood has seen eleven distinct migrations like this in the past quarter century. In this way, a ministry can keep the same focus, based on a particular need, but move from wave to wave.

As immigrants grow more accustomed to their situation, as they go further on the curve, their needs change. Soon they need English Language Learners classes, work readiness or driving lessons. They may have moved further away from the city's core or even to a second- or third-ring suburb. They are beginning to speak enough English that volunteers who speak only English can make an impact in their lives. They are moving to a point where they have firmed up a new "identity"—they have synthesized internally the new self in the new place. As they move to the right side of the curve, they grow in their ability to get beyond their immediate needs, build relationships and join groups. These folks, with whom you have already built relationships, can now begin to be brought together into Bible studies or house churches.

As time goes by, immigrants will move to more stable

neighborhoods, with better schools and buy homes. Often this means moving to a suburb. A ministry to a particular immigrant group may have to migrate with them! The kids we worked with in downtown Minneapolis twenty-five years ago now live in third-ring suburbs, have attended post-high school education, have jobs in the suburbs and yet still drive to the city to buy specialty foods and ethnic videos. Some return to our congregation, commuting in like our other suburban members.

Why Are Immigrants Drawn to Culturally-Specific Churches?

As folks become more assimilated, at the right edge of the curve, they may desire to join an English language multi-cultural congregation. These should probably be built not in the core city, but in the mid- to outer suburbs. I believe that most who join such a multi-cultural congregation are the children of immigrants, or immigrant children who grew up here. These 1.5- (born abroad but raised here) and second-generation children have much in common, with one foot in each culture. We have found that these kids are hungry to spend time with others who are also 1.5- or second- generation kids, even if their friends are from a different or even hostile culture, such as Hmong and Lao. They may be from different cultures, but they all understand what it means to belong to both cultures and neither.

However, few of the first-generation immigrants will want to come and join an existing mono-cultural, English language church. Even in the case of those more acculturated, even those living in the outer suburbs will want to attend an ethnic-specific church. Their cultural-specific church is a haven where they can worship in their heart language and spend time with people whose words and actions they do not have to decode constantly. Why will few first-generation immigrants feel comfortable joining your mono-cultural. English language church?

For a moment, imagine that starting tomorrow, you are going to be a member of the local Korean church. (For the sake of this example, you do not speak Korean.) You will have to worship in Korean. Pray in Korean. Know how to pray. Sing in Korean. Know when to stand up. You will have to enter that culture very deeply to feel you belong. You will need to know how far to stand apart when speaking to someone and with whom you are allowed to initiate conversation. You will have to know what subjects are politely broached. You will need to know how group decisions are made. You will need to know how to prepare the foods for the potluck dinners, how to eat them properly, and what sauces go with which foods. You will need to be able to understand and contribute appropriately in sensible language in Bible studies. You will need to develop the level of cultural fluency that will allow you to develop deep friendships and share your deepest needs.

How long would it take you to feel like you fit in? How long until you could attend a small group and speak heart-to-heart, faith-to-faith? One of our members served as a missionary in Senegal for 13 years. He has several advanced degrees. He is completely fluent in French and has a deep understanding of the Senegalese culture. Even so, he says that even after all those years he still feels like he can only truly worship in English.

Would the Korean church be *your* first choice for membership? How long would it take you to get to that level of cultural fluency, so that you could reach the point of intimacy and transparency? *That same challenge exists for every new immigrant who we hope will enter our churches.* Very few will have the ego strength, self-esteem, desire or even free time to make such an investment. For the first-generation immigrant, most will be drawn to a culture- and language-specific church, a place of refuge. That's why they're not attending your church.

An Acculturation Hierarchy of Needs

During the education process, many readers will have been acquainted with "Maslow's Hierarchy of Needs." Abraham Maslow was a mid-20th Century psychologist who developed this system, recognizing that people had to have their most basic needs met before they can move onto more complex and demanding psychological tasks.

Maslow's Hierarchy of Needs:

Self-Actualization

Esteem

Social

Safety

Physiology

In the same way, after an immigrant's basic needs are met, such as food, water, shelter and job, the next task is the re-establishment of one's identity. It is just as critical as the need for food, water and shelter. This task is complete when things feel normal again, and this new place feels like "home."

Culture shock is a function of identity; the human mind needs to figure out again, "Who am I?"

When people undergo change, whether it is the good

A Cross-Cultural Outreach Hierarchy of Needs:

- Meaning & Intimacy!

- Relationship/Respect
- Identity

- Job (Income)
- Shelter
- Water & Food
- Air

---

change of a new baby or a great new job, or bad change, such as a death or divorce, they inevitably go through a time of identity crisis. They have to figure out again who they are, as defined by this new place and new relationships. Working through this "stuff" makes the brain work overtime, and we call that depression. In most folks, after a few months, a bit more sleep, sometimes some odd dreams and feeling a bit out of sort, they come to a place where they feel "normal" again, this time in their new place. That describes the mechanics of culture shock, depression and identity.

Identity is the Key to Relationships

Until people have this new identity solidified, they are very little able to reach beyond their immediate needs. Once the basic physical needs are met, identity is the next issue with which they have to deal. Once (and only when) that identity issue has been settled, they are able to move on to create and sustain relationships.

Relationships are built on mutual understanding of culture and identity. Cross-cultural relationships cannot happen until I understand my culture and my identity and then have learned a bit about your culture

33

and your identity. Before you can build a relationship, you need to have your new identity settled, and learn something about my culture. To understand you, I must understand your culture and vice versa. This four-way connectedness makes cross-cultural relationships challenging and rewarding.

Relationships lead us to the place where the church is created to function—*intimacy*. Only when I get to the point where I can deeply share my inmost self can I reach intimacy and deal with deep questions of meaning. Intimacy is where the church functions as the church. Many monocultural congregations never get that far, so we can see how challenging it is to cross those several thresholds to get to the point where we can reach intimacy. People are extremely sensitive to differences when they face the challenge of developing intimacy. We typically best reach intimacy by being involved with people who share our culture and worldview to the greatest extent.

In 1977, Dr. Donald McGavran coined the term "homogeneous unit principle" (HUP). This is the concept that "birds of a feather flock together." If you desire to build a ministry, the easiest way to do it is to gather a group of folks who have a lot in common in terms of culture, worldview, ethnicity, socio-economic level, etc. The more these people have in common, the easier they will be to bring together into a church. The reason is that they find it much easier to shape a common identity and proceed to intimacy.

The Megachurch phenomenon has been built on the HUP. Typically, a church-planting team will study an area, and define a particular target audience, based on the demographics, above. They will then create a program and market that program to people of that one demographic group. Such churches have exploded across the growing American suburbs in the past 30 years. Even so, this model is very difficult to use when dealing with a multi-cultural congregation, because the HUP is not present. Where there *are* large *multi-ethnic* congregations, typically the core is made up of young, professional 1.5- and second-generation young people, who live in a particular area and share much of the same culture! They are one HUP unit, even though they look different from each other. They have much in common.

The HUP is not something to resent; it is as much a part of reality as our need for air. The key for those of us who desire to build the church cross-culturally is to recognize the reality that the HUP presents: We have to get to the point of understanding each other's culture and forge a common identity before we can move on to intimacy and meaning.

We Have Tremendous Sensitivity to Cultural Sameness

Let's look at this more deeply. I live in a first-ring suburb that touches the larger city; in it, there are about a dozen churches of my denominational heritage. They have developed through the past 75 years over against one another. One is a blue-collar evangelical congregation, now charismatic. Another is an energetic church-growth trendy congregation. One is intellectual and liberal. Another is intellectual, cool and conservative. Another is known for being wealthy. One congregation gets its identity from still fighting denominational battles of 40 years ago! Another is like a small-town, middle-of-the-road congregation. Another is conservative and strict. These churches claim the same theological heritage; many use the same hymnals and worship order! Nevertheless, they *feel* culturally different.

The bottom line is that people, mostly third and fourth generation Scandinavians and Germans all have chosen one of these churches because they perceive they will be comfortable there. It's a place they understand and can be understood. They are pretty much all politically moderate folks, living in middle-income houses. Prospective new members visit all of these churches; some join each of these churches every year. Even so, *prospective members self-select a congregation in my community according to micro-cultural clues as to heritage, theology, philosophy, socio-economic level and their perception of how well they fit in.* Although they all probably share 98 percent of culture, these differences are enough to make them feel uncomfortable. If the people in my hometown (and yours) can sense such tiny differences, and determine they could or could not be comfortable in a given congregation, what do we think people from another culture will think about joining your churches, when you probably share 50 percent or less of worldview, religion and culture with them!

For first-generation immigrants, the ethnic-specific, language-specific congregation is the most comfortable and efficient way to gather, disciple, teach and establish a Christian presence. If these congregations can be paired with a culturally-savvy existing church, whose people are well trained in and welcoming of the other culture, it may be even more successful.

Particularly, as children become fluent in English, Sunday School becomes a challenge as the immigrant parents do not speak English, and the children cannot read their parents' language. A joint English language Sunday School can be the fruit, and the paired church can develop a joint youth program that serves both cultures. Sharing is hard work; the hardest parts being the kitchen, storage space and an up-to-date joint calendar of who uses what when! The fruit for both groups is priceless. We have shared our building with a Latino congregation for more than a decade. When I count the handful of the most meaningful experiences of my life, like getting married or the birth of my sons, I count the partnership I share with that pastor. For the past couple of years, now four churches share our building. It has many challenges, and communication is critical. For many existing congregations, such relationships may be their only hope for a future, IF they are willing to share and *change.*

Expecting people from other cultures to flood our existing, monoculture English-language congregations when they come to this country seems terribly naive and improbable. But why *do* some join?

III. Degree of Acculturation Curve

Immigrants, due to things like education, self-esteem, life experience, ego strength, and many other factors, vary a great deal as to *what degree they become fully a part of their new culture.* My grandparents came from Norway speaking English. My grandfather was a skilled machinist and got a good job with the Great Northern Railway about 1908. They joined an English-language church and forbade their children to learn Norwegian. Even so, I now recognize many of my mother's

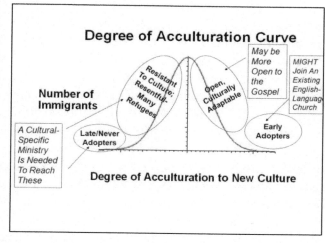

behaviors and attitudes being those of a child of immigrants: eager to fit in, obsessed with "that's what people do," proud of family heritage, patriotic to her country, very conscious of class, supportive of education, etc.

My grandparents readily jettisoned their Scandinavian homeland, if not their accents. They actively sought intense identification with all things of their new culture. They were "early adopters" of their new culture. In each migration, some will be early adopters. My secretary is Amharic Ethiopian; she married a Nigerian-American immigrant. They are both members of Anglo-cultural churches, by choice. They wanted an entirely "American" wedding. They are early adopters. The right tail of the curve would illustrate them and my grandparents.

Not all have the strength, courage, gifts, education or desire to go so boldly into their new culture. Most take great comfort from familiar language, customs, foods and other old cultural norms. Some feel resentment of the new culture and great grief at their loss of home. Remember, most refugees were forced to leave their homeland at gunpoint! Some adopt new forms readily and earlier than others do. A few never make the transition. A few blocks from our church is the "Norwegian Memorial Lutheran Church." They still have services in Norwegian weekly, to keep the culture, heritage and music alive. They celebrate their tradition, and welcome a few new Norwegians who come here for business, etc. The large Norwegian influx ended about 1910. I think we can safely call that church as being made up of "late adopters," as illustrated by the left curve of the tail.

Of course, many folks take comfort or pride in remembering their heritage. A couple times of year, we dine in a Minneapolis German restaurant, which is my wife's background. In our church's neighborhood, surrounded by over 1000 Latino and Somali businesses, is Ingebretsen's Nordic Marketplace. A hundred years ago the street it's on was the main commercial area for Scandinavian immigrants in Minneapolis. Folks drive thirty miles from the suburbs to buy their grandparents' simple peasant foods as precious delicacies. Around Scandinavian holidays, the lines are filled with polite but scowling great-grandchildren of peasants. They scowl, because that is what Scandinavian-Americans do when they are intensely involved or ecstatically happy. I always remember to warn guest preachers about that. Old Norwegians look like a tough audience, but when they lean forward and scowl, it means they are approaching ecstasy! Our churches each have a culture, don't they? Even third- and fourth-generation Americans can show their old cultural roots. As we seek ways to reach out to our new international neighbors, we need to be aware that we have a culture; we have many presuppositions about the smallest details of what it means to "fit in."

Applying the Curves to Ministry Planning

Looking at these bell-curves, we can see that a welcoming sort of ministry belongs in a "gateway" neighborhood, often in the core city[10]. As immigrants become more acculturated, they will move to other areas in a predictable pattern. They will be reachable by different kinds of ministry, aimed at their more-acculturated needs. In smaller cities and towns with labor-intensive industries attractive to newcomers, these same sorts of welcome ministries may be needed.

As immigrants begin the process, due to culture shock and their deficits in the most basic needs, they will find it hard to invest themselves into a community or even an ethnic congregation at that time. As they become more stabilized, able to turn outward, they are more able to congregate, develop relationships, and might have leisure time to spend in community, school or even church programs. As I said earlier, people on the left edge of the personal acculturation curve are people you "do ministry to." People on the right side are people you are more able to "do ministry with." To expect to bring non-Christians, part of a group of new immigrants from a distant culture into an existing English language church is not realistic in most cases. To begin with, pre-evangelism relationship building, based on their needs, makes sense. The relationships made may become deep and trust-laden. Faith can certainly be shared, but without knowledge of the immigrant's language, it is difficult. Resources such as the *Jesus* film in the newcomers' language can be good door openers.

As they become more acculturated, and begin to share a language with their welcomers, more opportunities for witness begin. English Language Learning or work-readiness courses can be good meeting grounds. As they become more comfortable, they will have fewer needs and there will be less opportunity to reach them with the Gospel. Ironically, as the task becomes easier, it simultaneously becomes more difficult. The importance of learning the newcomers' language, to be able to communicate early in the process, becomes clear.

Churches, according to their location, will have differing opportunities. The siting of ministries to these newcomers, as well as recognizing the stage they are in the acculturation process is critical. A good ministry in the wrong place or the wrong time is worthless.

Ministries must also be flexible to continue to be relevant.

The challenge of learning to reach our new international neighbors will be *the* challenge for the 21st Century American church. If we do not learn to reach them, the church will become a much weaker influence in society, and, our culture may become Balkanized. Let us pray the Lord of the Harvest to give us wisdom and understanding for the harvest at hand!

"John" is a Lao immigrant. He trained as a physician in China and the USSR. His father was a Lao air force general. His family escaped Laos, and North Vietnamese soldiers wounded him while swimming across the Mekong River. He has been here about 40 years. His English is not very good, and because his medical credentials are not recognized in the US, he works at a warehouse job. His wife works in food service. He became a Christian in Laos, and has wrestled here with his faith, because sometimes life has been hard. Their children struggled with gang involvement when they lived in Minneapolis, and his daughter became pregnant as a teen. Today she's a young mom with two children and is active with her family in building a Lao church in northern Illinois. The family is split between there and Minnesota. They have had struggles; they have had great heartache. They have grown in their faith and experienced many of the same challenges as any urban or suburban family. Our church served them for many years, and John even served part-time on our staff. They helped teach us about ministering to and with immigrant families.

These families are just people, like each of us. They are struggling with challenges of employment, education, learning a new culture, keeping their family intact and fitting in. They need the love of Jesus Christ and the love and outreaching arms of his Church. The future of our American culture will ride on how our people learn to reach out to these new Americans. What is your church doing to reach them? Where do you hear God's call?

As we begin the task of cross-cultural mission at home, what are we trying to accomplish? What does it mean to make a Christian disciple? How does one live in one's own culture to be a biblical believer? How much of our own culture do we need to reject in order truly live out our faith?

As we work with people from other cultures, what cultural norms and attitudes get in the way of a biblical faith? The roles of women and men? The way sexuality is lived out? Understandings of honesty and truth seem different than yours? Let's begin by looking at the differing ways that various American forms of Christianity approach the challenge of living out faith within their culture.

Chapter Three-
How Can We Do Social Ministry Without Losing Gospel Proclamation?
-A Primer on "Law and Gospel"

I) Historical Background:
The Liberal/Fundamentalist Split and the Rise of the Social Gospel

The mainline Protestant church began the 20th century at a time of great optimism. America was energized as it entered the global stage by its victory in the Spanish-American War, and having completed the Panama Canal after the French failure. Technologies such as electricity, the telephone and the internal combustion engine were highlights of the bright future promised by the World's Fairs at Chicago (1893) and St. Louis (1903). Christian theologians brightly spoke of bringing Christ's millennial rule, because the new machines of warfare, such as the repeating rifle, machine gun and breech-loading steel artillery made war too horrible ever to happen again. Optimistic writers spoke of the 20th Century promising to be the "Christian Century," which gave a name to a famous journal. The optimism is summed up by H. Ernest Nichol's 1896 hymn, *"We've a Story to Tell to the Nations:"*

> *We've a story to tell to the nations,*
> *That shall turn their hearts to the right,*
> *A story of truth and mercy,*
> *A story of peace and light,*
> *A story of peace and light.*

> *Refrain:*
> *For the darkness shall turn to dawning,*
> *And the dawning to noonday bright;*
> *And Christ's great kingdom shall come on earth,*
> *The kingdom of love and light.*

> *We've a song to be sung to the nations,*
> *That shall lift their hearts to the Lord,*
> *A song that shall conquer evil*
> *And shatter the spear and sword,*
> *And shatter the spear and sword.*

America was also developing a sharp social conscience, as women's suffrage and the temperance movement gained steam. Upton Sinclair's novel, *The Jungle,* which remains in print a century later, moved the hearts and minds of the nation, affecting labor conditions, the treatment of immigrants and the establishment of sweeping laws regarding the preparation of food in America. At this time, a young Baptist preacher began to write about the church's response to these social ills. Walter Rauschenbusch (1861-1918) became the father of what he called the "Social Gospel." His *Christianity and the Social Crisis* (1907) and later, *Theology for the Social Gospel* (1917) called the church to wake up to the ills around it, such as child labor, workplace safety, etc. His views are summed up with a quote from his 1918 work:

> The social gospel is the old message of salvation, but enlarged and intensified. The individualistic gospel has taught us to see the sinfulness of every human heart and has inspired us with faith in the willingness and power of God save every soul that comes to him. But it has not given us an adequate understanding of the sinfulness of the social order and its share in the sins of all individuals in it."[4]

He called this work of bringing justice through social change the "Social Gospel." This new call for awareness of and action toward social ills, coincided historically with the American church's beginning to deal with the critical biblical/theological issues raised by the Enlightenment in Europe a century before. The American church had been more resistant to Rationalism, biblical historical criticism and skepticism, but in the Reformed denominations, a split formed around that time between camps known as "Liberals" and "Fundamentalists." This split within the Mainline churches,

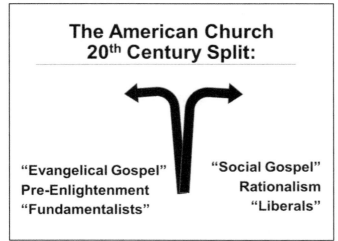

The American Church 20th Century Split:

"Evangelical Gospel"
Pre-Enlightenment
"Fundamentalists"

"Social Gospel"
Rationalism
"Liberals"

such as Congregationalists, Presbyterians and Episcopalians saw the Liberals fully embrace the Social Gospel as its central task, whereas the Fundamentalists, in reaction, rejected social involvement and embraced instead the personalistic Gospel of Salvation in the first third of the century.

The Leftward Shift of the Mainline Church

This split went on to affect the entire American church in one way or another. For the third quarter of the 20th Century, an unexpected outside factor created change in the church: the peacetime military draft. After the Korean War, all young American men still needed to register with the Selective Service System at their 18th birthday. If they were physically fit, the draft required them to serve for two years in the armed forces. If they wished to attend college or other accredited school, they could "defer" their conscription up to four years, as long as they kept a B average.

There were few ways to avoid this service; however *ministerial* students could avoid the draft by requesting a "divinity deferment." If they received one, they *never* had to serve, going directly through college and seminary to the parish. Regular college deferments kept students out of the Vietnam War only for the period of their studies at an accredited school; the divinity deferment was the only means to completely avoid having to serve. Throughout the '60s, thousands of young men on the anti-war left edge of American politics attended seminary in to receive this deferment. In 1969, deferments ended, replaced by a draft lottery for all young men. The result was stunning. Seminary enrollments plummeted; for example, at one Midwestern mainline seminary, the incoming class was half the next year.[5]

This huge influx into the Mainline American church's leadership of draft-avoiding young men with a leftward socio-political worldview had a tremendous impact on its direction and teaching. The final phase of this movement was the rising popularity of Liberation Theology in the 1970s. It was based on a melding of biblical content with a Marxist worldview and idea of history. Gustavo Gutiérrez' *A Theology of Liberation* is the best-known work of the movement; other noted writers included Jon Sobrino of El Salvador, Leonardo Boff of Brazil, and Juan Luis Segundo. This second wave of the social gospel taught that the Gospel says Jesus was always on the side of the downtrodden; therefore, God is always on the side of anyone who can claim to be a victim of oppressive powers; *that is justice.*

So, from the 1920s to the end of the century, in reaction to this rise of the Social Gospel and Liberation Theology, most of the Fundamentalist, Evangelical and Pentecostal churches became wary social ministry, because that was the concern of the Social Gospel and the Liberal churches. Because the Left understood the call of Jesus and the content of the Gospel to be the call to create social justice, the Right avoided it, attacked it, and feared delving into it, lest they lose the precious Gospel that brought people to faith. They rightly critiqued and feared how the Social Gospel destroyed the growth of the church, saw how the Mainline church ignored the propagation and nurturing of faith, causing the Mainline church to crumble even as its young firebrand pastors demanded more and more social action.

In the past twenty years, Evangelicals and Pentecostals have once again begun to embrace social ministry, on the historic lines of Jesus, Francke, Hauge, and Wesley. Indeed, Jesus' teachings on care for the poor and helpless are very clear and unarguably biblical. Yet, as I attend Evangelical conferences around the church, I am deeply troubled by the lack of theological awareness and clarity shown by the speakers. I am struck by the uncritical and naive way I hear the words of the '60s activists coming from the mouths of 21st century evangelicals, without them seeming to realize the content and direction of their words. Particularly, I am very alarmed at the prospect of Evangelicals following the mainline churches, giving up the evangelization of the world while pursuing social needs and political power.

Thus, trying to be biblically faithful when surrounded by immense human need, the key question for the American church is: *How do we do social ministry without losing Gospel proclamation?* By proclamation of the Gospel, I mean the historic sharing, preaching and teaching of the Good News about Jesus' life, death and resurrection, which leads to and empowers Christian discipleship.

II) Recognizing a Biblical/Theological Framework: Law and Gospel Tools from the Reformation

How do we do social ministry without losing Gospel proclamation? Interestingly, the Reformation leaders made the answer very clear. Both Calvin and Luther gave us good theological and scriptural tools. They give us a framework by which we can organize our thinking.

Particularly looking at Romans, Luther saw that Paul recognized a very useful scriptural dichotomy between "Law" and "Gospel," or in the Old Testament, the Hebrew words *"mishpat"* (justice) and *"chesed"* (covenant love). Paul recognizes two different *functions, actions* or *structures* of Scripture at work. These are not a question of Old versus New Testament, but God's Word *functioning* in two very different ways from Genesis to Revelation. If we understand these two functions, differentiating between their two very different goals and outcomes, we can easily understand the two different aspects of all Christian ministry.

One Function of Scripture: The Law, With Two Uses

The first function Paul and Luther call "Law." The Law, as seen in the Ten Commandments and moral law of the Old Testament, reflects the order God has created in the Universe. God has created laws that are the design by which all reality, the entire Universe functions. God created the Universe with an invisible, but discernable framework of scientific and moral laws that invisibly govern at all times and places, whether we recognize them or not.

First Use: Order Everywhere We Look

Studying his Bible, especially understanding Paul's thought in passages such as Romans 1-3 and 7-8, Luther recognized that the Law has two *uses*. God's Law has two ways in which it works in our world and lives: The first use is to create *order*. God created the Universe in order, and so his laws govern all the processes and relationships, the very reality of the Universe. When God speaks in the very beginning, his Word is, "Let there be light." The Universe comes into being, and all the laws of the Universe come into being at the instant of that Big Bang. We can see the Law create order in things like the laws of science; the whole Universe functions by them. God's moral Law and the laws of science are all evidence of the Mind that created the Universe and keeps it running in harmony. God speaks, and his Word creates order; the Law comes into being at Creation. God's order keeps the stars in their courses and makes it rain on the just and the unjust. The Periodic Table of the Elements, the way all of matter works and reacts, is the same all over the Universe. The Periodic Table works the same today as when I was in high school chemistry or on the first day of Creation. The laws of gravity or thermodynamics are true whether I accept them or not. We can even speak of "chaos theory:" even in the midst of chaos we can find an order![2] There is hope for my desk!

Everywhere in Creation, we see beauty and order. We can see that there are many small fish and a few big fish. If the big fish eat too many little fish, then there will be fewer little fish; then the big fish will starve off, keeping balance. As the little fish increase, soon there are more big fish, and all stays in equilibrium.

We can look at the mighty forces of nature and see that they are understandable. We can see that the laws of science mean that the sun shining on a warm prairie causes the air to heat, which results in great storms, and their tornadoes can cause great damage. We can understand the forces, and even predict their outcome. We can see order in Creation. We also know that order is only created by a Mind. My desk never cleans itself; it takes an organizing mind to create order. If a child comes home from school and finds her messy room is now clean, she knows it did not clean itself. The orderly mind of Mom was at work. All of nature, by itself, moves toward minimum energy and maximum randomness (enthalpy and entropy); mountains wash down into valleys; complex molecules break down to more simple compounds if left to themselves. Organization to a higher level only happens by outside intervention. That is the Second Law of Thermodynamics. It is true everywhere in the Universe. We can look at this order and power and perceive that there is a Mind behind it—*but,* nature never tells us if that power *loves* us. It is always a cold, impersonal force at best. From the beginning, God's Law creates order.

The Law as Structure: Invisible and Absolute

Another way to think about the Law is that it is the structure of how the Universe works. It is the invisible framework of all of existence. The Law is part of Creation, simply the structure of how God created Creation, including people, to function and interact. God's order controls the Universe from sub-atomic particles, to chemical reactions, to the movement of galaxies, to human morality, framework within a framework, within a framework, from the smallest to the whole. Because of sin, we are always bumping into that invisible Law, bruising or breaking ourselves. Because of sin, we can't fully understand right from wrong, nor can we do more than some good. Because of sin, we can neither know God nor do his will. When we run hard into the Law, it's not that God is out to get us, or smash us; it's just the outcome because of sin. We can't see it clearly, but for some reason we revel in breaking it, dashing ourselves against it.

I remember an event at our Boy Scout camp years ago. Our troop loved to play the game Capture the Flag, but when we played it, it was sort of Lord of the Flies meets WWIII. We played very hard, and of course, in complete darkness. That year we were in a heavily wooded campsite of about ten acres. The road into the campsite ran right down the middle, so we used that as the no-man's-land between the two sides. It was a dangerous strip, because the other team could catch you out in the open and drag you off to jail. Therefore, to be successful in invading the other team's land, you had to get across the road quickly. Did I mention that this was in the woods? And nobody could use flashlights? It wasn't just a little dark; it was pitch-black.

We had a fast little guy, Scotty, who was a particularly reckless player. He would put his head down, shoot across that road, and often find the other team's flag. We were playing capture the flag one cloudy night, when there were some quick footsteps on the road, and then a big thump. Ever hear the sound of a watermelon being dropped? After a pause of several seconds, we learned what the thump was. Somebody yelled, "Hey, Scotty hit a tree. He's out cold."

That tree was not out to get poor little Scotty. That tree was not being mean. It simply had grown there. It was part of the structure of the woods. Scotty just didn't pay any attention to it. He ran into it headfirst, and he, indeed, was knocked out cold.

Thus it is with the Law; the Law is just the structure of how God created the Universe to work- but because of sin, we cannot see it. We can't reason it clearly. All people have some awareness that we need rules to keep ourselves out of trouble. That's what Romans chapters one and two are about. All peoples, all nations, all philosophies have some form of the Ten Commandments; all have some built-in sense of right and wrong, but we keep running head-first into the Law. Why? We can neither understand it clearly nor do fully what it demands. Like Scotty in the dark, we can't fully see or understand the Law's demands. Our thoughts and feelings lead us into a selfish, rebellious existence, where what we want drives us into more and more blindness.

The First Use Creates *Offices*

Another part of the Law's creating of order is the creation of *offices*.

In all cultures, at all times, we see that there's the *office* of something like a king, prime minister or president; in all cultures there is a policeman, there are judges, teachers, parents, soldiers and even executioners. This is God's good gift to create order. All of these exist because God's moral law is written in all human hearts, as Paul writes in Romans, chapter 1, and humans create these structures everywhere. Invisibly, God maintains order by the invisible gift of the Law. When an atheistic Communist police officer in China arrests a speeding motorist, whether she understands her actions as such or not, she is part of God's invisible rule in the Universe. She too is enforcing God's moral Law.

God's Law is the invisible structure that links all of reality together. Yesterday, at least six out of seven billion people had enough to eat. What an amazing structure God has invisibly created in this world! Think of the toast you had at breakfast. How many people made it happen? They all did work so that they also had something to eat. What an amazing system of interdependence, all based on the need to eat!

Your toast began as wheat planted in North Dakota. A huge John Deere tractor tilled and planted that land. Its tires began at a rubber plantation in Indonesia. It was carried on a freighter with a crew from around the world. The rubber was unloaded by dockworkers, carried by truck and tractor to a tire factory where skilled hands made those tires. The tires were made on machines made by thousands of other people. There were light switches in that plant; other workers provided heat and light. Then there was the steel in the tractor, and copper, and plastic, and computer chips made by a chain of thousands in China. The farmer also owns a huge combine and many other pieces of equipment, touched by a chain of tens of thousands of hands.

The wheat was tended by that North Dakota farmer, then trucked to the grain elevator, loaded on a train and milled into flour in Kansas City. That truck and train were built, maintained and fueled by thousands of other people. The flour was put into bags made by other hands, and shipped to a bakery closer to your home, who made the bread, put it in a bag made of oil from the Mideast, and you popped it into a toaster made in Korea. You ate it on plates made in Japan, on a table from Sweden. How many people's work interlinked to make your toast possible this morning? Two million? More? That's all part of this incredible structure of the law that stretches from the tiniest part of creation to the greatest.

When all is in order, when all have justice, then everybody eats.

There is enough food in the world to feed everybody. The problem is in the places where the system breaks down. Where things are in order, *(zedek)* then there is justice *(mishpat)* and God's invisible law, working in an invisible way keeps order all over the Universe, whether we realize it or not. When some take shortcuts, then children are not fed, sewage is dumped into rivers, people are cheated, and some profit unjustly, the same as in Amos's day. Sin is when people break the Law; then the system breaks down.

We can break the Law; we can get rich by stealing, and many do. We think we can end our problems through killing; but the law says that killing only begins your problems. We think we can make our life better by lying, but that also destroys us. The Law, as revealed clearly in God's Word, is there like a fence to keep us away from running head-first into the structure of the Universe and dashing our brains out on it. Another illustration is that the Law is like the fence on the side of the freeway— it's there to protect us from getting hurt, or hurting somebody else. It *does not* tell us where we *should* go. It simply keeps us from going where we *should not* go. Keeping order is what 16th Century reformer Martin Luther calls God's First Use of the Law.

Order: The Left-Hand Work of God

This keeping of order, so that the Universe and humanity can continue to exist, was called by Martin Luther the *left-hand Kingdom of God*. In Isaiah 28:21, the LORD is describing how he is going to intervene violently to bring judgment, and he says: *[21]For the Lord will rise up as on Mount Perazim; as in the Valley of Gibeon he will be roused; to do his deed—strange is his deed! And to work his work—alien is his work!* The work of the Law is God's alien work, his work of judgment and order.

Parents don't decide to have children because they want someone to punish! Parents have children so that they can love and nurture them. That's the great thing of being a parent and a family: the love, the nurture and the common shared life together. Occasionally parents have to step in and discipline children, because children need to be directed to things that are good for them and others. I did not look forward to disciplining my children. I didn't like disciplining them, but if I hadn't, I would have been derelict in my duty; their lives would have been ruined as well. They could have turned out as monsters.

So it is with the Law; punishment and judgment are alien to the central work of God, which we will look at next; even so, through the Law and its enforcement, God makes the world orderly. Laws are just, people are treated fairly, people are fed, lakes are kept clean and the world functions. Order: that's the first use of the Law. It's simply recognizing how the Universe works. Order, as it brings structure and offices: that's the first use of the Law

Second Use: Drives Us to Christ

As human beings, all societies and cultures have rules. These have developed so that human life may be sustained on this planet. Paul tells us in Romans 1-2 that the reason all peoples have these rules is that God has created humans with these rules written inside them. All peoples have some version of the Ten Commandments.

However, as we try to live in harmony within that Law as it guides our society, as we try to live in harmony with our family, as we try to be righteous or just, all humans fall short. All the world religions are built on the struggle to change our "self;" to live in harmony with moral law and even a way to find forgiveness or salvation from the demand of the system in which we always fall short.

If we struggle to live in harmony with or obey the first use of the Law, if we attempt to do everything right, we soon come to a point where we realize that we can't make ourselves good enough to do the things we know we ought to do. We are broken. The harder we try to keep the law, the finer it grinds, so that the harder we try to obey it, the harder it becomes. That's the second use of the Law: it drives us to Christ. The harder we struggle against the Law, the more it knocks away all of our excuses, all of our claims, and naked the law drives us to the mercy of God. Our inability to be good leads to an understanding not only of our culpability in our relationships, but ultimately that we stand as unjust before the Universe and its Creator. This becomes a religious question that all world religions try to fix. We come up short. This is not a fun thing. The Living God of the Universe desires to strip us of our self-centeredness, our smug sense of "I'm pretty good" and anything we would use to justify ourselves. The Law accepts no excuses, which is exactly what we need.

We see this moral law of God in Scripture, like the Ten Commandments. Here I think our perception of God and God's Law is warped. Perhaps we picture God, the Moral Judge sitting over the Universe, in perfect holiness and justice, just waiting for some poor human being to do something wrong—then, -splat- God gets 'em. Certainly the Bible presents God as the Righteous Judge, but 'not vindictive nor capricious. Hebrews 10:31 says: *"It is a fearful thing to fall into the hands of the living God."* Indeed, God is righteous, and we are not. God cannot allow into his presence anything that is not righteous and holy. What does it mean to be righteous before this universal Law? The most basic meaning of the Hebrew word *(zedek)* "righteous" means to "be the way it was created to be."

Dr. Joseph Sittler, the Lutheran theologian, gave this illustration in a lecture many years ago. He was visiting Israel, driving an ancient car. The car began to misfire, so they stopped in the next village to see if they could find a mechanic. The mechanic checked a couple of things and wiped out the distributor cap. He started the car, and it ran right. He closed the hood and proclaimed, *"Zedek!"* It once again was the way it was created to be.[ii]

Therefore, to be righteous is to live, to be in the relationship with God that you were created to be in; however, sin has warped us, and made it impossible to do or even know all of the moral Law.

As we try harder and harder to do the right thing, particularly as we realize that we know we *should* do the right thing, the more we realize that we cannot. We try harder. We fall short. We may even realize that there is a just God, and we want to deserve to be forgiven before God. Nevertheless, the harder we try, the harder the demand becomes. We finally realize that the law is like a 500-foot-high smooth granite cliff we cannot climb. We have no ability to fulfill it perfectly, and the harder we try to be good, the more we realize the level of our brokenness. Like falling onto a millstone, the Law grinds us finer and finer.

The Law puts limits on our old nature and works at killing off that old nature. Paul describes it in Romans 6:6—*We know that our old self was crucified with him so that the sinful body* (self) *might be destroyed, and we might no longer be enslaved to sin.*

Paul talks about the tension between these two natures in Ephesians 4:22-24—*Put off your old nature which belongs to your former manner of life and is corrupt through deceitful lusts, and be renewed in the spirit of your minds, and put on the new nature, created after the likeness of God in true righteousness and holiness.*

Yet the Law and its demands can never create anything. It only limits and kills. The *Gospel* is the *power of God.* Let's focus now on the other *function* of the Word of God: The Gospel. The Law kills; the Spirit, working through God's Word of the Gospel, brings life.

III) The Gospel & Salvation: God's Central Purpose & Right-Hand Work of God

What is the Gospel? Paul explains it very well in Romans 1:16-17 and 3:22-24—

> *I am not ashamed of the gospel, because it is the power of God for the salvation of everyone who believes: first for the Jew, then for the Gentile. For in the gospel a righteousness from God is revealed, a righteousness that is by faith from first to last, just as it is written: "The righteous will live by faith."*

> *This righteousness from God comes through faith in Jesus Christ to all who believe. There is no difference, for all have sinned and fall short of the glory of God, and are justified freely by his grace through the redemption that came by Christ Jesus.*

What is the Gospel? It is the story, the Good News of what Jesus has done for us, taking our sin upon himself on the cross. It *is* the message of the cross. It is centered on John 3:16: *For God so loved the world that he gave his only begotten Son, that whoever believes in him will not perish, but have everlasting life.* When we hear what Jesus has done, the Holy Spirit works through that story and creates faith inside us. The Bible tells us (Rom. 10:17) *"Now faith comes by hearing, and hearing by the message of Christ."*

The Gospel *is* the power of God to create this faith-life inside of us. The Gospel thus is the power of God to give us new life, to create a completely new nature in us, one that loves God and neighbor and led by the Spirit, wants to obey God and do the right thing. Paul sums up the action of the Gospel in Romans 8:1-4:

> *There is therefore now no condemnation for those who are in Christ Jesus. For the law of the Spirit of life has set you free in Christ Jesus from the law of sin and death. For God has done what the law, weakened by the flesh, could not do. By sending his own Son in the likeness of sinful flesh and for sin, he condemned sin in the flesh, in order that the righteous requirement of the law might be fulfilled in us, who walk not according to the flesh but according to the Spirit.*

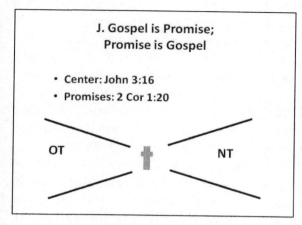

J. Gospel is Promise;
Promise is Gospel

• Center: John 3:16
• Promises: 2 Cor 1:20

OT   NT

All the promises of the Bible, those Old Testament promises pointing toward Christ beforehand, and all the New Testament promises explaining him afterward, all *function* as Gospel. *Gospel is promise and promise is Gospel.* That is the second and primary function of Scripture. *Christ* and the Cross are the center of the Gospel; Paul says, *"All the promises of God find their Yes in him."* (2 Corinthians 1:20) The Holy Spirit, working through promises of God's Word *creates* the reality of those promises in us. God builds a new us, in us, through his Gospel promises coming alive in our lives like powerful seed.

The Gospel is the chief work of God, the normal, central work of God. Since the beginning of God's salvation history, God has broken into the midst of this structure of the Law to create something greater, covenant love *(chesed.)* The New Testament calls that action the Gospel. The Gospel alone creates the new being in us. This is why God sent Jesus. The Law is there to keep order by limiting and killing our old nature. The Law drives us to Christ. Both Law and Gospel are God's action among humans; both are driven by and unified by *love.*

The Christian struggles with both the work of Law and Gospel inside of each of us. Notably, when Paul speaks of the tension of our old self and new self in Romans, chapters seven and eight, *both* are written in the present tense. Our old nature hates God, rebels against God, seeks to use neighbor, manipulate God and serve only one's self. The new nature loves God, loves neighbor, and is obedient to God; that self is a new self, created in the image of Christ by the Holy Spirit working through the Gospel.

When our boys were little, they would hop in the back seat, and we would head off to Pizza Hut or Yellowstone Park. It did not matter if it was ten minutes or several days; at some point things in the back seat would reach the point where I would hear myself saying, "OK, if you don't settle down back there, I'm pulling this car over..."

The purpose of the trip wasn't for me to be the Hanging Judge. No, the purpose was something good, like supper or a vacation. To get to where we needed to go, we needed to get those in the back seat there... alive. Thus, although I was the loving Daddy, taking our family for a treat or a fun time, to do good to my children, my alien work was to enforce a bit of law and order. God's entire good purpose toward humankind is to bring us back into a relationship with him. His central work is to save us. That's the "right hand" main work of God, but his alien work, "left hand" work is to keep law and order so we don't destroy ourselves.

Now please understand, the Law is not God being mean and the Gospel is God being nice. Both Law and Gospel are something far greater—both are love in action. If you see your four-year-old reaching up toward the stove, about to pull a scalding pan of water down on herself, you scream and grab her away, so she is not killed or terribly hurt. You do not worry about hurting her feelings— you need action to save her life. So it is with the Law; God loves you so much that he desires to protect you. Thus, God's Word functions as both Law & Gospel.

To summarize, the Law creates order and drives us to Christ; through its God creates his invisible, left-hand rule of Law; God is invisibly in control of the Earth through the Law. *The earth is the Lord's and the fullness thereof...*" (Psalm 24:1) God invisibly maintains his rule in this "left hand" kingdom of order through the Law.

The Gospel creates faith and a whole new being inside of us; this is the right-hand, central work of God through Jesus Christ. The Gospel alone creates another kingdom, the Kingdom of Christ, which rules in the hearts of individuals now, and will come in its

Summary: Two Functions

LAW:	GOSPEL:
1) Creates Order	Creates New Self
(Limits Old Self)	& New Obedience
2) Drives Us To Christ	
(Kills Old Self)	
- Order, Offices, Punishment; Invisible Structure	-"Right Hand" Kingdom of Christ
-"Left Hand" Kingdom Of This World	- Invisible Now; Fullness at Christ's Return
- "God's Alien Work" (Is. 28:21)	- The Power of God
- Part of Creation – Pre-Dates OT & NT	- Central Task of the Church
Basis of "Social Ministry" = JUSTICE & ORDER	Re-establishes RELATIONSHIP With God

fullness when Christ returns. These are the two functions of Scripture, each ruling in a separate sphere. The Law produces justice and a civil righteousness. The Gospel creates faith, creates a new being in each believer, creates a new reign in each believer that looks ahead to the coming of Christ's perfect kingdom at his return. This is how these two separate functions of God's Word work in human beings so that God's will can be done on Earth. These themes run through the length and breadth of Scripture, not just in Paul's writings. A bit further down we'll look at the development of Biblical language to describe this relationship in the Old and New Testaments.

IV) The Law and Gospel in Practice: *Chesed* Love

Thus, when we talk about social justice, that's a function of the Law. Justice (Hebrew *mishpat)* is a function of keeping the moral Law of God. God likes order. That's a function of the Law. God desires people to be fed, God likes rivers to be clean, he likes all his creatures to be cared for, to have justice for the weak, to limit the power of the strong, to make sure children are educated, for water to be clean and so on. As we read the moral law in the Old Testament, as well as the words of the prophets, there is a very clear message of doing the Law. The *Torah*, the first five books of the Old Testament sketch out ways in which God's Law should work out in humanity.

Here is the critical point: Our *relationship* with God is the center of both testaments. Our relationship with God is always a function of Scripture functioning as Gospel. In the call of Abram, God comes and makes a seven-fold promise to Abram before he does anything else: (Genesis 12:2-3)

> *(1) "I will make of you a great nation,*
> *(2) and I will bless you*
> *(3) and make your name great,*
> *(4) so that you will be a blessing.*
> *(5) I will bless those who bless you, and*
> *(6) him who curses you I will curse, and*
> *(7) in you all the families of the earth shall be blessed."*

More broadly, how do these themes play out through the Bible, and what is their scriptural basis?

Understanding *Chesed:* Covenant Love

God creates the covenant with Abram in Genesis 12. This unilateral choosing by God is the key characteristic of God's character in both Testaments. God reaffirms his covenant love towards Abram in Genesis chapter 15, but Abram cries out that God still has not given him any of the promised offspring! God responds by telling Abram to cut several animals in half, and to lay the pieces in two lines. Abram recognizes this as a covenant treaty, late Bronze Age Fertile Crescent suzerainty treaty. When a greater king conquered a lesser king, the losing king would be forced to pledge his allegiance to the victor, enacted by the loser walking between the dead animal pieces. The message was clear: you break this treaty, and you are dead meat.

The amazing surprise of Genesis 15 is that as Abram waits, *God, not Abram, takes the loser's walk!* God, as a flying fire pot and torch passes between the lines of dead animals. God takes the penalty of the covenant! The God of the Universe pledges himself to Abram and his descendants in this covenant of blood. *This is the message of the cross, 1800 years early! God takes the penalty and creates the covenant.*

Throughout the Old Testament, a very special Hebrew word describes this specific concept of *covenant love* being acted out here. The Hebrew word is *chesed.* It is *the* central theological word of the Old Testament, and yet, because it is not translated consistently, we can't always pick it out in our English Bibles.

To help to understand this interplay between Law and Gospel, let's look at a surprising place, Micah 6:8. Throughout the '60s and '70s, this verse was a favorite of the social activists:

> W*hat does the Lord require of you*
> *but to do **justice*** (Heb. mishpat),
> *and to love **kindness*** (Heb. chesed),
> *and to walk humbly with your God?*

I have normally heard this explained that God simply wants us to be good and be nice. Is that all Micah is saying? No, these words are profoundly deeper than that. These words illustrate the deepest truths and function of Scripture.

Jeremiah links these words in a central passage, showing the same relationship:

> *[23] Thus says the LORD: "Let not the wise man boast in his wisdom, let not the mighty man boast in his might, let not the rich man boast in his riches, [24] but let him who boasts boast in this,*

*that he understands and knows me, that I am the LORD who practices **steadfast love, justice, and righteousness** in the earth. For in these things I delight, declares the LORD."* (Jeremiah 9:23-24 EHV)

Nehemiah makes the link between covenant, *chesed* and *mishpat* (keep his commandments) *[5] And I said, "O LORD God of heaven, the great and awesome God who **keeps covenant** and **steadfast love** with those who love him and **keep his commandments**, (Nehemiah 1:5 EHV)*
Let's go on and see how these words play out.

Do *Justice;* Love *Covenant Love*

Justice *(mishpat)* means to keep, to do, the moral law. To keep the moral law, to be the way God wants both us and the world to be, is a part of righteousness *(zedek)*. It is based on being in the *chesed* covenant. It's based on the moral law, as explained in the Old Testament first five books and spoken about in the prophets as well. There, laws about marriage, keeping contracts, punishing criminals, boundary lines, inheritances, property ownership, money lending and even rules about not over harvesting wild birds are all spelled out. These are part of God's moral Law. To *"do justice"* is to live according to those precepts, to live in harmony with the Universe as God has created it and revealed it.

The difficult concept is the next one. We are called to "love kindness." "Kindness" is a very poor translation of the underlying Hebrew word, *chesed*. Let's see why.

The original text of the Old Testament was in Hebrew. *Chesed* in Hebrew describes a relationship of covenant faithfulness. It describes the attitude of the LORD to his people, which is a covenantal relationship created and gifted to individuals and nations as a gift. *Chesed* means "covenant love," based on the promises and the faithfulness of YHWH, the LORD.

The relationship of Abram to the LORD, which was imposed in Genesis 12, is a *chesed* relationship. In various translations, *chesed* is translated into English as lovingkindness or steadfast love; it's also translated as "mercy," "grace," and "kindness." We are going to find that the content of the word *chesed* is the same reality as what Paul calls *Gospel,* a bit further on.

The action of *chesed* can best be described by a parabola, like a big

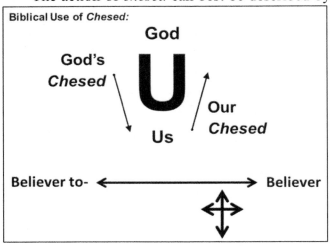

U or a McDonald's arch turned upside down. It is an action that begins from above, from God, comes down to us, and creates a response back toward God. God's love and grace towards us are described in the Old Testament as *chesed*. Our response to God's faithfulness and love is our response of love and faith, created and empowered by the *chesed*-love-grace of God. That's what the word *chesed* means, but we've lost that meaning because there is no single Greek, Latin, French or English word that covers all those meanings, the way the Hebrew word *chesed* does. Because of that, we can't see the amazing continuity of thought between the Old Testament and the various New Testament writers.

In Micah, the 6:8 the ESV translates *chesed* as "kindness." Why is there such confusion? Let's look for a moment as to how the Bible came into English. About 200 BC, the Old Testament was translated into Greek, so that its message could be heard by more Jews, who had already been spread around the Mediterranean by the Babylonian destruction of Jerusalem in 586 BC. The story goes that this translation was done by a group of seventy scholars, so it was referred to as the Septuagint, often abbreviated "LXX."

Chesed: A Problem of Translation
(We Have Lost the Meaning of *Chesed!*)

Heb → Gk → Latin → Old French→Old Eng. → English

Chesed	Eleos	Misercordia	Mercit		Merci		Mercy
Covenant Love Grace, Faithfulness	Grace, Mercy, Compassion		Favor, Pity, Reward for Showing Pity	Reward, Gift, Kindness	Compassion, Forebearance		Pity!

As these scholars tried to translate *"chesed,"* there was no single Greek word that completely translated the various meanings of grace, love, covenantal love, mercy, kindness, patience, faithfulness and trust. So, in the LXX, the Greek Old Testament, *eleos,* meaning mercy and more, is most often used, as well as other Greek words for love and grace. Yet, as *eleos* was used, generally, the rest of the meaning of the word was lost.

In the mid-fifth century, when *eleos* was translated into Latin by St. Jerome, the underlying *chesed* lost more of its meaning. When the western church began to use the Latin Bible, most of the meaning of *chesed* was permanently lost. In Latin, the word became *misercordia,* meaning favor, pity, or even a reward for showing pity.

(There is a curious hint at the challenge the church faced in transmitting the meaning of *chesed* into Latin. In the Latin mass, just one section is in Greek, not Latin. That section, *Kyrie eleison,* the cry of the lepers, asking Jesus to remember God's covenant with them, becomes the only part in the Latin mass to remain in Greek! Why? There seems to be a memory that *Eleos* picks up part of the meaning of *chesed,* which would be almost lost with the Latin *misercodia.)*

Later, as the word entered old French as *mercit,* it was taken to mean reward, gift or kindness. With the Norman invasion in 1066, Old English adopted that word, *merci,* where it came to mean compassion or forbearance. Thus, the word *"chesed,"* a rich word meaning covenant love, grace, and faithfulness morphed into our modern word, "mercy," a word that means "pity."

Thus, we begin with a majestic word meaning the grace-filled, covenant-love, empowering concept, which is the center of Old Testament thought, and even the center of Temple worship as seen in innumerable Psalms, and end up with a wimpy word that captures about two percent of the word *chesed's* original meaning, leaving us with pity. Therefore, with the words *"I desire* chesed *and not sacrifice,"* Hosea is calling the people of his day to return to the passionate covenant relationship, created by YHWH's promise. Matthew twice quotes these powerful words to show that Christianity is the true continuation of the Old Testament faith. 6

To sum things up, thus, when Micah says,
>*What does the Lord require of you*
>*but to do justice* (Heb. mishpat),
>*and to love kindness* (Heb. Chesed),
>*and to walk humbly with your God?*

Micah is calling God's people to the historic three aspects of God's relationship to his people:
- To live and do just things according to the moral law,
- To love the God of the covenant, who had first extended that covenant-love *chesed* to them, and

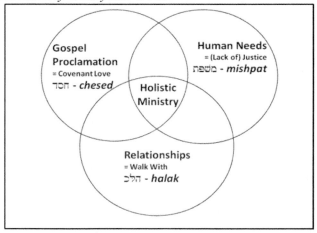

- To humbly walk in a relationship with each other and their God.

As I mentioned above, the distinction between *mishpat* and *chesed* can also be seen in Jeremiah 9:24: *But let him who boasts boast in this, that he understands and knows me, that I am the LORD who practices* **steadfast love, justice, and righteousness** *in the earth. For in these things I delight, declares the LORD."*

The connection of *chesed* and covenant are visible throughout the Old Testament in verses such as Nehemiah 1:5 *And I said, "O LORD God of heaven, the great and awesome God who **keeps covenant and steadfast love** with those who love him and keep his commandments.* An exhaustive study of these words is beyond the scope of this little book, but the definition is covered in many standard Bible dictionaries and commentaries.

Chesed in the New Testament

When we look at Matthew, his Greek and Aramaic speaking audience seemed to understand the importance of this *chesed* word. Matthew is a very spare writer. If we compare his accounts to Mark or Luke, he always tells the same story in a stripped-down version. If Matthew were asked to describe himself in 25 words or less, he would have answered, "Concise." He is not one to repeat himself. However, with this quote, he does repeat himself, using it twice, to emphasize this important concept in his Gospel. Matthew is writing to a Jewish audience within the context of the destruction of the Temple. Sacrifice was no longer possible; the Pharisees were the only other Jewish sect left standing, and they taught that God must now expect us to keep the law, which meant following their interpretation, traditions and expanded ordinances.

Nowhere else in the New Testament is Hosea 6:6, quoted, except in Matthew. It says,

> *For I desire steadfast love* (Heb. *chesed*, Gk. *eleos*) and *not sacrifice,*
> *the knowledge of God rather than burnt offerings.*

Matthew quotes that verse twice. Once at his own call (Matthew 9:13) and again at the end of a sequence—something greater John the Baptist...Jonah...Solomon and the Temple and its sacrifices. (Matthew 12:7) That is where Jesus quotes Hosea 6:6 the second time:
And if you had known what this means, 'I desire mercy, and not sacrifice,' you would not have condemned the guiltless. The relationship with YHWH, reestablished by Jesus, was greater than the sacrificial system of the Temple. He is greater than the "Temple" and all it stood for.

At the time of the writing of his Gospel, Christianity is contending with the rise of Rabbinic Judaism as to which will be the path for the Jewish people to follow. Matthew is making the argument to his readers that Christianity is indeed the true continuation of the Old Testament faith, the continuation of the *chesed* relationship, which is its basis. The old sacrificial system had been given to Moses as way for living that *chesed* relationship out. Now the Temple is destroyed; the Temple is no longer needed. Jesus has fulfilled the law; Jesus himself is the fulfillment of God's continuing action with his people. His attitude and working are the same: *I desire* chesed, *and not sacrifice...*" The continuation of God's relationship with his people is fully summed up by Hosea:

To do *mishpat* is to walk within the moral structures of the Law.

To love *chesed* is to respond to and live in the covenant love relationship YHWH has established for his people.

And to walk (sustain a mutual relationship) humbly together with their God.

Paul and John Find Other Words for the *Chesed* Concept

In the rest of the New Testament, the writers struggle with the

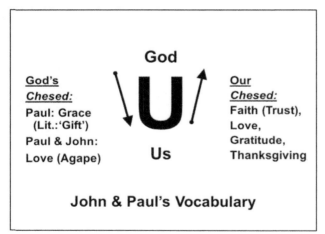

untranslatable nature of *chesed* and so find other words to describe the same reality. In the illustration, we see the parabolic nature of *chesed,* symbolized by the large "U." The left side shows God's action, *chesed.* The right side shows our response of *chesed.* To describe God's action of *chesed,* Paul uses grace[7] (Gk. *charis*, one of the LXX words used to translate *chesed)* or *agape* love. To describe the human response created by God's action, Paul uses both faith, (believing, trusting) (Gk. *pistuo),* and *agape* love toward God.

John uses the word grace only (Gk. *charis)* four times in his gospel, all in the first chapter, to connect his thought with Paul's writings. He never uses the term *charis* again in his gospel. Instead, he simply speaks of God's action as *agape* love, and our response as love or believing.

So, where do we see this idea of *chesed,* reciprocating covenant love in the New Testament? Each time, think of the descending and ascending parabola:

- 1 John 4:19- We love, (both God and people) *because* he first loved us.
- Ephesians 2:8- For by *grace* you have been saved through *faith*; and this is not your own doing, it is the *gift* of God
- Romans 5:8- But God shows his *love* for us in that while we were yet sinners Christ died for us.
- John 3:16- For God so *loved* the world that he *gave his only Son*, that whoever *believes* in him should not perish but have eternal life.

The human-to-human aspect of the *chesed* relationship is a New Testament norm as well, as evidenced by many other verses, including:

- Ephesians 4:32- *Be kind to one another, tenderhearted, forgiving* (literally, "gracing") *one another, as God in Christ forgave* (literally, "graced") *you.*
- 1 Corinthians 1:4- I give thanks to God always for you because of the *grace* of God which was given you in Christ Jesus
- As we reflect on Paul's Law-Gospel thinking in Romans, we can see it as a reflection of the entire Old Testament's use of

Summary: Two Functions

LAW:
1) Creates Order
   (Limits Old Self)
2) Drives Us To Christ
   (Kills Old Self)

- Order, Offices, Punishment; Invisible Structure
- "Left Hand" Kingdom Of This World
- "God's Alien Work" (Is. 28:21)
- Part of Creation – Pre-Dates OT & NT

Basis of "Social Ministry" = JUSTICE & ORDER

GOSPEL:
Creates New Self & New Obedience

- "Right Hand" Kingdom of Christ
- Invisible Now; Fullness at Christ's Return
- The Power of God
- Central Task of the Church

Re-establishes RELATIONSHIP With God

mishpat/chesed. In fact, everything Paul describes as the action of the Gospel can be summed up in the OT use of *chesed.* This Law-Gospel dichotomy is particularly reflected in the simple formula Hosea gives us:

What does the Lord require of you
but to do justice (Heb. mishphat),
and to love kindness (Heb. Chesed),
and to walk humbly with your God?

Therefore, we see that idea of the two functions of God's Word, Law and Gospel, flow through the entire Bible. Like the two mighty cables that hold up the Golden Gate bridge, these two themes provide the major structure in Scripture, illustrating God's activity toward humankind. The concept of covenant love that the important Hebrew word, *chesed*, describes continues its influence into the New Testament. The New Testament writers use other Greek words to try to describe it, such as *eleos* (kindness/mercy/covenant love), *charis* (grace), *pistuo* (believe, faithfulness), *agape* (agape love) and *euangelion* (gospel-good news). As we look at what Paul and Luther described as Gospel, we see the totality of what the Old Testament describes as God's action of *chesed*. This is the steadfast, covenant-love/grace extended by God, based on God's covenant, created by God's action, completed on the Cross.

How Do We "Do Justice?"

Thus, to "do justice" is to make things right, the way they are supposed to be. To be involved in true "justice issues," is to help to do the things that Scripture teaches us as feeding the poor, having justice which is impartial to both poor and rich, enforcing justice and contracts, keeping the civil peace and even caring for Creation. However, these are NOT the Gospel; they are the Law. God has given us the good gift of the Law, and the Holy Spirit changes us to live in harmony with each other. The Law limits our behavior, convicts us of our sin, and puts our old nature to death.

The Holy Spirit working through the Gospel creates a new, deeper obedience in us, a whole new nature in us, that gives us the power to live in harmony with the Law by the higher obedience created by the Spirit working through the promises of the Gospel.

Therefore, we as Christians are called to teach and preach the Law. We are called to work in the secular realm of government and political action, as individuals, to create a society that obeys the law and strives for justice.

The Church is called to teach the Law, right from wrong, according to the teachings of the Old and New Testaments. We teach the ideas, concepts and principles. We teach God's Word. Rational thought can help us work through what the Law means; Scripture does not work out for us how to interpret each commandment in every setting. When Scripture teaches: *Deuteronomy 22:6 "If you chance to come upon a bird's nest, in any tree or on the ground, with young ones or eggs and the mother sitting upon the young or upon the eggs, you shall not take the mother with the young"* we can deduct from this a whole array of laws regarding the environment and our relationships with the species we've been given to care for. It is not spelled out for us; rational thought gives us tools to wrestle out, to interpret what this means in each time and place. However, our rational thought about justice does not negate or overpower God's moral law. A "justice issue," no matter how dear to our hearts or political platform cannot disagree with God's revealed moral law. It is always our rock and source; it judges us.

Working it Through in a Democracy

How does this all work in a democracy? Doing this interpretation, as a society, is difficult. When the law tells us to care for the poor, supporting widows and orphans, that teaching may look very different to us as individuals. In a democracy, each of us have one vote. Each one comes to the political process with one vote. Each church member may take the Scriptural teaching, and see it a bit differently, according to their life's lens.

That teaching may be understood very differently by a widow living on the Social Security minimum as compared to the small business owner drowning in taxes. Another church member may be a wealthy inheritor of great assets. Another is a student graduating with $100,000 in college debt. Another is an abandoned single mother, trying to raise two children and create a life for her little family in their two-year lifetime window of welfare support. What is justice? Who can afford what? Who should pay for what? How do we create support without creating dependency, taking away self-worth or destroying the family?

Each of these people will hear God's Word command us about supporting widows and orphans.[8] Each will wrestle with that truth in their hearts and minds. Their church should teach them and guide them in interpreting that Scripture. They then take their understandings and convictions to the caucus, the newspaper opinion page, to their blog, the water cooler at work, and to the ballot box. This is the work of God, through humans, in the Kingdom of the Left. In our American democracy, we each partly hold the office of king. We work politically and vote according to what we learn from God's Word. Individual Christians, Christians working through organizations and Christians working in political parties should boldly be about bringing justice, as they understand it. They may differ in their opinions; that is the method of a democracy.

However, very, very, very rarely should the church intrude as a power broker in this Kingdom on the Left. When it does, it rarely serves the Gospel well. The Church's central role is the central role of God in Christ: creating the Kingdom on the Right, the Kingdom of Jesus Christ, by preaching the Gospel. Jesus says his Kingdom is not of this world. Neither Jesus, Paul nor the other disciples sought to wield political power in the name of Christ or the Church. Paul *did* use his citizenship as a tool for witness, which is quite different, using it to appeal all the way to an audience with Caesar.

When the Church begins to flex political muscles, when the Church grabs political power, we can quickly end up with things like Calvin's Geneva where people were soon being burned at the stake in the Name of Jesus. We could say the same of the Inquisition. When the Church wields political power, the Gospel is always compromised.

Rarely the Church Must Lead in the Alien Political Realm

There are rare times when the Church is called to step into the political realm of the Kingdom on the Left. These are those times when Scripture is clear, and a believer, for the sake of the Law or Gospel, cannot not speak. Those times are very, very rare, and often end up sullying the reputation of the Church and its ability to share the Gospel. The Reformers said that such an issue had reached the level of *status confessionis*— confessional status, where faith intersects the political realm. Any time we suggest we have certainty in such an issue, we are entering the realm of Law, politics and the Kingdom of the Left. It is an alien, messy sphere for a church, as the whole Church.

At this point in our historyhave, our congregation believes that only one issue consistently reaches that point, the issue of abortion. We have discussed it; we have looked at it carefully theologically; we have looked at the costs to our proclamation, and finally, reluctantly, we have entered that debate. We have also always said that if we are to be pro-life, then it also seems biblical that we must be pro-woman, pro-child and pro-family. Working out those details is hard. We also approach the topic with the greatest tools we have, those of the Gospel: grace, love and forgiveness, for those who face or who have made this decision. Those are our central concerns. Even so, we thought and felt that the Bible was clear on this issue, and our church should publically speak.

The role of bringing justice by wielding political power should remain at the point of the Christian as citizen. Believers are taught the same Bible by their church. Each believer weighs and interprets those words by their conscience, and continues to learn and wrestle with Scripture. They then take their understandings and work them out at work, in advocacy organizations such as PETA, AARP, the Sierra Club or NRA, in the political systems and the ballot box.

Justice Issues That Do Not Divide

Some justice issues can be addressed by the church directly and not be divisive. Christians can address these without making the Church a secular power broker and enter into an alien realm. This is the realm of servanthood. People need food. Homeless people need shelter. People need to learn the language of their adopted country, and how to read. Many of these issues are things Christians can agree on and reach into that human need. Those are the areas where we have a clear biblical call, and can be used as a blessing and point of commonality with our neighbor. In this book, in our simple method, we will call those "access points."

These are the places, even the God-prepared places, where human need intersects each of our lives. Each of us has much we can give away to neighbor, without cost. It might be how to speak English or read; it might be how to wash clothes in a machine, use those funny porcelain objects in the bathroom, walk on ice for the first time, drive a car, use a computer or raise better soy beans. These ministries may be tiny; a couple of friends decide to reach out to a local apartment complex and form a soccer league, get to know the kids and share Jesus. A small group of retired teachers at a church sees a need for an ESL program and reach out to Latino immigrants in their community. A baby Latino church is the fruit five years later.

The purpose of our method is to change the self-awareness of the member in the pew, from being a religious consumer demanding more and more services to a new awareness of being a front-line missionary, individually fulfilling the Great Commission *and* the Great Commandment simultaneously. All of this can happen without direction from the Pastor or church leadership. We find congregation members spontaneously creating micro-ministries, with no funding and no costs, that meet the very heart of immigrants' needs, create relationships and bring the Gospel.

We would do well to listen to the voice of the political left wing of the Church, and listening, judge their agenda by the voice of Scripture. There *is* a call from Scripture to love and serve our neighbor; there is a call for believers to do justice. However, this does not mean we give up proclamation to do it! This does not mean that any particular group who considers themselves downtrodden or oppressed, simply because they feel sad or who can't have their way, is necessarily on the side of God. If behavior that Scripture disallows is the thing that causes the group to be rejected, they cannot claim discrimination as a "justice issue," if what they desire breaks God's moral law. Something that is unjust cannot be made into a "justice issue" no matter what a culture or denomination believes at the time.

> Thus, as we look at ministry, we see that God's Word calls us to
> -do justice, to
> -love the covenant-love, (Gospel-faith relationship with God and)
> -to walk humbly together in relationship with each other and our God.

We will look further in future chapters as to how these three aspects can come to be lived out in the life of your congregation and your community.

Chapter Four
A Continuum of Six Responses to American Culture

<-- Disengaged ----------- In the World But Not of the World----------- Enmeshed-->

1 Outside of Culture	2 On Edge of Culture	3 Parallel Xn Culture	4 Evangelical but Involved w/ Culture	5 Cultural Christians	6 Secular Culture
Cultish groups who have virtually no contact with the surrounding culture.	*Typical US Fundamentalist. Having very little contact with outside world- but not "cultish".*	*Typical US Evangelical approach--a parallel "Christian" universe, not much different from mainstream.*	*Typical US Evangelical or turned-on Mainline Christian.*	*Typical US Protestant Mainline Mirrors social beliefs and standards of culture.*	*Total identification with and participation in their portion of US culture.*
Amish & Christian Utopian Societies & Communes	"The World" is mostly a place to work, shop, etc. Culture is distrusted and seen as alien.	Popular "Christian" Schools-- Strong Christian focus, but patterned greatly after public schools-dances, clubs, etc.	Strong Christian identity, but involved in culture, at cost of sense of separation. Critically using structures of culture to reach culture	Acceptance of cultural norms in arts, entertainment, etc. -- "political correctness"	Increasingly hostile to most forms of Christianity
Jehovah's Witnesses	Kids in home schooling, small Christian academies; distrust of "Christian" schools and public schools	Parallel organizations such as "Awana's" or "Pioneer Clubs" modeled after Scouts.	Attending public schools, self-consciously as Christians; speaking up in class and learning to be bold in hostile culture. Kids on front line can be at risk. Teaching in public schools as form of witness and ministry.	Tries to bring some form of "Christian witness" in society, but with little focus or idea of what is uniquely Christian	There are many "secular cultures"- no longer one standard, American, "TV culture."
Inability to speak to or--reach culture because of no contact with "regular people"	Distrust of secondary education; perhaps small, ultra-sectarian Bible schools with sense of "chosen few."	Emphasis on private "real Christian" Christian colleges.		Tends to mix social agenda of political fashion, left or right, and see it as identical to "Christian" agenda.	"Political correctness," secular multiculturalism, being inclusive and being non-judgmental are seen as the greatest cultural goods.
Attractive to people who desire to be "different"--often feel disenfranchised or unacceptable	Tendency to see very narrow group as "saved"- often those of small cult-like group or sect.	"Christian" psychology and counselors	Involvement in community groups such as Lions, 4-H & Scouts as channel for evangelism. Typical approach of missionaries when approaching a new culture.	Society's agenda of "being nice" at that time dictates ethical teaching of church and agenda of its policies.	"American Civil Religion" used to dominate our American culture, but that has been replaced with a new secular piety based on relativism and non-judgementalism are the norm.
Appeals to people who want an absolute authority and do not want to deal with their society	Political views may be a bit eccentric; various conspiracy theories, etc.	"Christian" cookbooks, knick-knacks, Bible verse or Christian imagery home decorations, paraphernalia, etc.	Unafraid of study of secular psychology, medicine and science, but done critically with Bible as highest authority.	Attempt to live daily as Christians within society, but uncritically and accepting of most current trends.	Religion, especially if it impinges on behavior, is seen as unacceptable and "mean."
May appeal to maladjusted people, for whom being a part of a "persecuted" fringe group fits into their personality and view of reality.	Worship-only traditional, organ-only, or liturgical or traditional "gospel" music only --defined as music from particular era that spawned group, or even rules of no accompaniment.	"Christian" pop music	Use of media, arts, fashion all within cultural norms, with Christian conscience, to "fit into"	Celebrate Christian holidays, have church membership, but rather inarticulate in witness and understanding of faith.	It is debatable whether or not one could be a Christian and not have any sense of differentiation from any culture.
Dress or customs may separate members vividly from surrounding culture.	Approach to society much like "hippies" of 60's- "tune in, turn on, drop out."	Acceptance of much of culture, but mirroring it in a "baptized" way.	Acceptance of much of culture; little attempt to build parallel "Christian" culture, instead tries to be critically open to using culture as a way of witness.		
		"Christian" dating apps			
Typically, very ineffective to outreach to community.	*Distrust of and lack of contact with outside world limits ability to reach culture in witness. Culture itself is seen as the enemy.*	*More able to speak to culture, but yet very little touch with society, often unable to find areas of witness contact with culture.*	*Attempt to be culturally fluent but faithfully Christian.*	*So enmeshed in culture that it may have little ability to be critical, work for change; discipleship is hard, as lure of anti-Christian culture is powerful from within and there is little sense of "otherness" or Christian identity.*	*Here, there is an uncritical acceptance of whatever cultural beliefs are prevalent.*

Chapter Four: A Continuum of Six Responses to American Culture
How do I Approach Another Culture?

The first page of this chapter has a rather complex chart. The rest of the chapter will explain it. The basic question as we evangelize a different cultural group is, what will that cultural group look like after the Gospel takes hold.

I was surprised to notice that much of what separates the various forms of American Christianity is how much involved in or separated from the surrounding culture. So, if a newly evangelized person is to live in their community, what will it be like? Will they have to entirely break from their culture? Can they continue to live, unchanged, in the cultural/religious milieu in which they were raised?

So, if we are to disciple a person from another culture, what is our target? Will that person have to be exactly like us? The same priorities, views on relationships with the family or the opposite sex? As the Holy Spirit grabs hold of a person's life, each individual from each family and each culture will be different from anybody else. Even so, what is to be our model?

As we approach another culture, to try to learn it and build relationships with its people, we will encounter many things that puzzle us, such as: Why are the relations between women and men defined as they are? Why does a person say yes when they mean no? Why is that person not looking me in the eye? These topics are too great for a book like this. They are better covered by an excellent text like Patty Lane's *A Beginner's Guide to Crossing Cultures*[11].

Yet, as we learn these differences, we will also come to find that each culture has patterns, just as our American cultures have. They are eager to learn to navigate what they perceive the culture around them, but they are bewildered because they see so many American sub-cultures with so many contradictions.

Each of us as American Christians also deal with living out our faith in the midst of our surrounding culture(s). Jesus' teaching on this has often been summarized that we are to be "In the world, but not of the world." What does that mean? Every culture has many wonderful, whole, just and life-giving aspects. Every culture also has destructive, binding, life-destroying, demeaning aspects and values. Paul's letters are full of instructions to the early Church on how to live in a sometimes-hostile surrounding culture. Letters like those to the Corinthians, in part, are teaching them how to live faithfully, surrounded by a culture with different values concerning idols, the roles of men and women and sexual morality.

Further, as we look across the continuum of how American churches live out being "In the world, but not of the world," we see that there are many answers. In fact, the difference between denomination types is often more a question of their stance toward their culture than of their interpretation of Scripture!

Before we begin to disciple immigrants or plant a church, we should first look at our own presuppositions of how Christians should relate to their culture. Should the way *we* approach *our* culture be the model that all immigrants use to approach their culture and ours? Are there things in an immigrant culture that may seem alien to us, but do not necessarily conflict with the Bible? Are all of the cultural presuppositions that we make appropriate for them, in their culture? Let's begin by each of us looking at our own stance.

A Continuum of Response
In the chart at the beginning of this chapter, the heading says, "In the world, but not of the world." Below it are six categories of responses, on a continuum, made by Americans as to what that means. Columns one and six are separated from the others, as I don't think these are valid Christian responses. Column one is to be radically separated from culture; column six is to be completely enmeshed. From left to right each position becomes one of greater acceptance and entrance into that culture.

Readers probably will not find themselves completely described by any one of these positions; most people represent two or three in how they have decided to relate to their surrounding culture. As you read these, pause and reflect on how you have responded in these areas, and why.

1. Outside of Culture
This position is typically that of cultish groups who have virtually no contact with the surrounding culture. These would be groups like the Amish, various Christian utopian societies like the Shakers, or cult-like communes. They teach that to live an authentic Christian life, one must pull entirely and vividly away from the surrounding culture. To a lesser

degree, this is true of the Jehovah's Witnesses, with their refusal to celebrate holidays or serve governmental duties.

People with this stance toward culture show a great inability to speak to or reach culture because they have no contact with regular people. A drop-out cult may be attractive to people who desire to be different, often wounded people who already feel disenfranchised or unaccepted. This kind of structure seems to appeal to people who want an absolute authority and/or do not want to deal with larger society. It may even appeal to maladjusted people, for whom being a part of a persecuted fringe group fits right into their personality and view of reality.

In order to enforce and display their separation, dress or customs may separate them vividly. This also gives them a deep sense of identity and group cohesion. The bottom line is that they are typically very ineffective to outreach to community.

2. On Edge of Culture

The first column inside the valid Christian response I term, "On the Edge of Culture." This has been a typical US Fundamentalist position, one of intentionally having very little contact with the outside world, but not to the extent of being cultish. For this group, "the world" is mostly a place to work and shop. Surrounding culture is distrusted, seen as alien, and to large degree as the enemy. How is this lived out?

For education, kids may be in home schooling or small sectarian Christian academies. There might be a distrust of public schools and even popular Christian schools, because they are seen as too worldly. There may be a distrust of secondary education, perhaps offering small, ultra-sectarian Bible schools with sense of a chosen few. The need for education is seen as primarily Bible knowledge, equipping for jobs in the church or for the development of independent small businesses.

For these groups, there is often a tendency to see a very narrow group as "saved," often those of small, almost cult-like group or sect. It has been my experience that these churches may have an unwritten shared political view, which may be a bit eccentric, such as various conspiracy theories or end times teachings.

The worship is sometimes idiosyncratic to the group, such as only traditional instruments, or liturgical or traditional gospel music--defined as music from the particular era that spawned the group. They may have rules of no accompanying instruments. The group may adhere to the

King James Version as they only valid translation.

Their approach to society is much like "hippies" of 60's: "tune in, turn on, drop out." For them, their distrust of and lack of contact with the outside world limits their ability to reach their surrounding culture in witness. Culture itself is seen as the enemy.

3. Parallel Culture

This is a typical stance of US Evangelicals. The approach is to create a parallel "Christian" universe, not much different from the mainstream. It's not too alien for those who wish to become believers, but it's still separate from what they perceive as "the world."

This would be the case for the large, popular Christian schools; they have a strong Christian focus, but are patterned greatly after public schools, with dances, sports teams, and clubs.

Instead of joining the secular Boy or Girl Scouts, they might join parallel Christian organizations such as Awanas, Boys' Brigade or Pioneer Clubs, modeled after Scouts. Their children attend private Christian colleges where they study typical college majors with other young Christians, and it's a place to find an appropriate, believing spouse.

Secular psychology is distrusted, but instead an openness to "Christian" psychology like James Dobson. Christian bookstores are filled with the "stuff" of the parallel universe: "Christian" cookbooks, Christian knickknacks like "Precious Moments," even rulers and pencils need Bible verses, and at the cash register it's not secular candy, it's "Testa-mints."

Christian pop music sounds a great deal like the rock and roll of five years earlier. Many love songs to Jesus are hard to tell if they are aimed at God or a boyfriend.

This position finds acceptance of much of the surrounding culture, but mirroring it in a baptized way. The bottom line is that they are more able to speak to culture, but have very little touch with society, often unable to find areas of witness and contact with their culture.

Evangelism for this group and the previous always has some sense of the need to pull people out of their culture.

4. Evangelical, But Involved with Culture

This is a typical position of many US Evangelicals or articulately faithful mainline denomination Christians. It is marked by a strong

Christian identity, but involved in culture, at the possible cost of a sense of separation: Critically using the structures of the surrounding culture to reach that culture. The groups to its left would see this approach as being too worldly.

For example, this would mean Christian children attending public schools, self-consciously as Christians, speaking up in class and learning to be bold in hostile culture. This puts kids on the front line, where they can be at risk. This would include Christian teachers teaching in public schools as form of witness and ministry. This stance might include involvement in community groups such as Lions, 4-H and Scouts as channels for evangelism.

Interestingly, this is the typical approach of missionaries when approaching a new culture. They learn the culture, and go as deeply into it to make relationships and bring Jesus. Even so, parts of every culture are broken, and so great discernment is needed.

These folks might be unafraid of study of secular psychology, medicine and science, but done critically, with the Bible as highest authority. Their use of media, arts, fashion would all conform more with cultural norms, but with Christian conscience, to fit into culture as much as possible.

This stance would show acceptance of much of the surrounding culture, with little attempt to build parallel "Christian" culture. It instead tries to be critically open to using culture as a way of witness. It is an attempt to be culturally fluent but faithfully Christian. The danger is to enter culture so far that one can become lost there.

5. Cultural Christians

This is typical of many US Protestant Mainline believers, or in areas in the Bible Belt or strong Roman Catholic communities, where little distance is recognized between living as a faithful Christian and the surrounding culture: Christendom. In this category, religion mirrors the social beliefs and standards of the culture. It means acceptance of cultural norms in arts, entertainment, etc. It would accept the local values of "political correctness" of left or right.

It tries to bring some form of Christian witness in society, but with little focus or idea of what is uniquely Christian. It tends to mix its religious practice with the social agenda of political fashion, left or right, and see it as identical to "Christian" agenda. Society's agenda of "being nice" at that time dictates ethical teaching of church and agenda of its policies, especially on the left.

There may be some attempt to live daily as Christians within society, but uncritically and accepting of most current trends, celebrating Christian holidays, having church membership, but rather inarticulate in witness and understanding of faith. These are culturally captive Christians, and nominal Christianity. This position is so enmeshed in culture that it may have little ability or desire to be critical and work for change. Discipleship is hard, as the lure of anti-Christian culture is powerful from within and there is little sense of "otherness" or any distinctly Christian identity.

6. Secular Culture

I would suggest that this position is again a non-Christian position. It means total identification with and participation in the surrounding culture. In the church, these could be Roman Catholic, Evangelical, Fundamentalist or Mainline people who are nominal Christians. Being a part of a church is just a civic duty and a part of the culture of that community. It could also be a church that has developed a form of Christianity so comfortable in its culture that it sees no difference, like American civil religion. This reflects a large part of the growing "unaffiliated" segment of our population, the unchurched.

If we were to represent this position within the Christian church, the idea here is that culture and society have set the agenda for the church, completely. No sense of any separation or difference from culture, nor of any need to differentiate self from general culture or the part of culture one feels is one's own. This will vary from culture to culture. Southern culture might include "love it or leave it" conservative secularism, or in blue color communities, unionism, etc.

It is debatable whether one could be a Christian and not have any sense of differentiation from culture. Here, there is an uncritical acceptance of whatever cultural beliefs are prevalent.

Summary

So where did you find yourself? How are Christians to live within a culture? That's the rub. There is no one simple answer, but most of us do not think that question through very often. We join a congregation, and that congregation has an unwritten set of dos and don'ts that we gradually learn. Certain behaviors and lifestyle choices are accepted, some are looked down upon. Most are cultural traditions and many have changed in the past generation. These cultural values, often without looking at any biblical basis, are a part of any congregation's culture. In the past 75 years, these have included the role of women, women working outside the home, appropriate worship styles and instruments, openness to social or political action by the church, and a million other things. On some of these things the Bible is clear; most are statements of values passed down as unwritten rules by those trying to live faithfully at a given time and place. We have to be very careful that in living out the Gospel, we don't confuse it with a human-concocted law.

When we reach out to a person of another culture, what do they have to learn, adopt, or give up to be a disciple of Jesus? What happens to the Somali's second wife? What happens when you learn that spousal physical abuse of women is a norm in a particular culture? What happens when the new believer of another culture can't understand why your church doesn't just share all its wonderful construction paper or disposable diapers with an immigrant partner church; don't Christians share? When is an event organized *enough?* What do you do when you're dealing with two churches of two different cultures, and the two have very differing senses of time, ownership and what *organized* means? What presuppositions are we making about their culture? How much do we have to follow our cultural norms for an event or shared experience to be "right?"

Do forms of music, national holidays, medical practices and culturally determined roles for women and men have to match our American Christian norms? Why or why not? These are questions and puzzles that you will need to solve constantly. Keep the continuum, above, in your mind as you disciple immigrants. Often the things you find frustrating will come from cultural presuppositions that we bring to what it means to be faithful, in our culture. Other cultures' faithfulness may look and act very differently. How much of our culture do we bring with us, and how does that shape our expectations? Keep that in mind as we move forward.

As we reach into a cultural group to design a holistic three-part ministry, how can we keep our thinking and actions sorted out so that we do not leave out one of the three aspects? How do we keep from getting so bogged down in these immense needs that we forget that we started out to make disciples?   What's the difference; isn't it enough just to do good?

How do you start?   How can you begin to interact with an immigrant people group and be effective?   How can you avoid the pitfalls of ignorance that doom many immigrant outreaches before they begin?   The next chapter proposes a simple method to learn a people group and find God's access point.   That is the topic of our next chapter.

Chapter Five:
Using a Four-Step Plan to Reach a Local Unreached People Group

In earlier chapters, we looked at patterns of how immigrants enter, learn and move. How can we begin to plan a ministry to a particular group or need? Over the years, our Mission*Shift* Institute has developed one simple system for learning about a given group in a given neighborhood. In class, we call this unit the "Unreached People Group Project." Although we give it to the students as an exercise, from it have come many start-up ministries that have touched many lives. After graduation, students have taken this simple method and used it to create ministries in their own neighborhoods.

Is it the only way to create a cross-cultural ministry? Of course not. However, it does show the kinds of things you or your group need to learn to be effective in outreach.

Learn or Fail

Having now served thirty years in the same core-city, multi-cultural neighborhood in Minneapolis, I have seen many ministries come and go. Hundreds of excited, Spirit-filled, energetic people have heard the call of God and came to our neighborhood to make a difference. I would guess that about 95 percent fail and give up within a matter of two years. Almost all of them fail either because they think they have all the answers or because they do not take the time to learn about their surroundings and/or the people they minister to.

It is beyond the scope of this book to give an overview of all of the factors that affect ministry in a given place. Suffice it to say, that no matter in what neighborhood you do ministry, several questions have to be asked incessantly: Why are things the way they are? Where did it come from? Where is it going? In thousands of ways, neighborhoods are affected by economic changes, real estate values, cash flow into or out of the area, tax policies, banking policies, political changes, political decisions like zoning priorities or siting of institutions, ethnic groups, transportation patterns, organized crime, and employment. The area is still affected even by things like where the jobs were 100 years ago, (which still affects the housing stock) where the street car lines were, the location of toxic waste areas and much more.

The same kind of background study needs to happen to begin to learn the culture, distinctive traits and history of each different people group.

We have over 100 languages in our two-square mile neighborhood. These may have several sub-groups; for example, there are dozens of distinct Latino groups in our area. Each of these possess a different culture. So, what kinds of questions do we need to ask to do the kind of background work we need to do to avoid failure? Hold that thought.

Before that, we need to look at our presuppositions about ministry; they will determine our outcome. Here are ours:

Our Presuppositions:
1) God Has Something to do With Billions of People in Motion Around the Globe *and* God Wills to Bring Them to Salvation in Jesus Christ.

In Paul's speech in the Areopagus, the Holy Spirit tells us something about today's global migration:

(God) made from one man every nation of mankind to live on all the face of the earth, **having determined allotted periods and the boundaries of their dwelling place,** *Acts 17:26*

Whatever is going on in this quickly changing, globalized world, God is in the midst of it. Paul tells us that in some hidden way, God is behind the movements of all peoples. If that is so, this is not a random happening, but somehow God is fulfilling his purpose in and through this amazing time. I think of the many groups that live as my neighbors who are from the "1040 window," that part of the globe between ten degrees and forty degrees north latitude, across north Africa, the Mideast and Asia, which represents the most difficult parts of the world for Christians to minister in. I could never go to these, but many of my neighbors are now from there! These people are from countries to which I could never travel and witness in, places like Afghanistan, Somalia, Tibet, Bosnia and Iraq. Hundreds of the highest-level Chinese academics and future leaders study at the University of Minnesota. We can reach some of the most unreachable people in the world, right outside of our door! Can we perceive God's action? God has brought these difficult-to-reach people right to our neighborhoods and workplaces!

2) Targeted Ethnic-Specific Outreach Is the Most Efficient Way to Begin Outreach to A New Immigrant Group That Does Not Have English Fluency.

Each word in that title was carefully chosen. Think through each clause.   In Heaven, there will be one Church, of every tribe, tongue and nation.   For the time being, unless there is a breakthrough, like if instant translation by smartphone is perfected, congregations for new immigrants will remain monolingual and culturally specific.   Even if instant translation becomes perfect, immigrant culturally-specific congregations will still be popular, as islands of comfort and familiarity in a new land.

3) The Current Needs/Situation of an Immigrant Population Offer an "Access Point" for the Gospel Via Holistic Ministry

Using our holistic ministry model, we believe we should not separate human needs from a person's need for faith. (Nor should human needs be divorced from sharing the Gospel!)   A human being has needs that are physical, emotional/intellectual and spiritual, because they are made up of body, mind and spirit.   The needs of an individual can be an important part of building relationships and reaching the whole person.

South Korea gives us a great example of this holistic approach to ministry.   The Yoiddo Full-Gospel Church in Seoul, is the largest congregation in the history of the world, with about 800,000 members. The central life of the congregation resides in house churches, which have as their main strategy to simply look for hurting people, surround them with love, help them with their needs, and bring them to know Jesus.   It's simple, bottom-up and inexpensive.   More importantly, it works.

4) You Will be Most Successful if You Define Your People Group as Sharply-Focused as Possible as to Group and Need.

You need to be well-focused in your outreach.   If you try to learn to do outreach to every conceivable people group around you, you can never succeed.   In our neighborhood, we have many people groups and so many needs!   In those groups, there is great variety; some have an education, some have none; some are young, some are old.   Some of our neighbors are chemically dependent or mentally ill.   Some are far along the acculturation curve, and others have just begun.   Some have come with wealth; some have nothing.

Many things may divide us.   People from India have a deep inward sense of historic caste differences, which are very hard for them to ignore. People from various areas or tribes of a given country may have a long history of friction and will have a hard time being served by the same program or church.   As much as we may feel sad that sin has caused such division among humankind, we also can recognize the reality of things that separate us.   Even outspoken Republicans and Democrats, with their differing worldviews, may have a hard time associating closely together in one church.   Every family knows the challenges those differences bring around the holiday table, even if those folks are the most closely related of all!

You are not going to be able to meet every need of every member of even one particular people group; you are not going to meet even one common need of all people groups.   Focus: if you aim at nothing, you will hit it every time.   If you aim at everything, you will hit nothing.   We have found that to be most effective you need to find a focus, some group that is big enough to be an adequate ministry target, and well-defined enough so that you don't have to constantly deal with cultural differences.

One of our Mission*Shift* Institute groups started studying Latinos in our neighborhood to find God's access point.   As they studied and learned, they finally narrowed it down to young, single, Andean (Ecuadorean, Peruvian & Bolivian) males, ages 18-30, who are chemically dependent.   These males had a lot in common, they had a severe unmet need and a shared culture.   No one was yet in a position to work with them, so the team's project led to the simple creation of an AA group in Andean Spanish.   Another group started with Somalis in general, and ended up with Somali single moms, with limited English, who lived in a specific neighborhood.   They planned specialized ESL classes to meet their needs.

Another group, all from one congregation, started looking at the needs of people living in a low-income housing project in their first-ring suburb.   As they studied the area, they realized that Latino kids were slipping through the cracks in the school system, needed tutoring, and had no access to Spanish-language recreation.   A member of the congregation lived there; her apartment became their base.   Later the complex gave them a rent-free apartment because their work was so valuable.   They built a simple after-school tutoring program, accompanied by a soccer program.   Now they are considering a Spanish-language worship service for their church.

Each plan was successful because they learned thoroughly who it was they sought to serve, they discovered what they had available to give away without cost, and they targeted their work at a very specific audience, so they were effective.

5) Proclaiming Jesus Christ is The Reason you are Going to Build all you are Going to Build. It May Involve a Great Deal of People-Care, but Proclamation of the Gospel Must be the Center.

The central purpose of God is to bring humanity back into a relationship with himself through Jesus Christ. Faith in Jesus Christ and a relationship with God are the greatest gifts we can bring to any human. If the church forgets that, or gets sidetracked from that, we have forgotten why we exist. At the same time, we do not minister to people in a vacuum. Jesus loved, healed and fed people. So did the apostles. As we face a society of broken people and broken institutions, we constantly face a world that has become broken. We need to deal with this, to the degree we can, as we covered in the earlier chapter, but if in doing so we lose the proclamation of the Gospel, we have failed.

6) Everybody Has Something They Can Give Away Without Cost That Somebody Else Desperately Needs.

This is a key ministry principle. Starting ministry to immigrant people does not take a budget of thousands of dollars. It does not need a full-time staff. It does not mean expensive buildings or investments. It does not need to rely on the pastor who cannot even find enough Sunday School teachers, who will collapse in tears if you say he or she needs to develop a cross-cultural ministry!

Our program is built on training the member in the pew to build small, bottom-up, short-term ministries that they can sustain with a few hours of effort each week. You might call these hobby ministries. By studying a well-defined people group to find the "access point" God has prepared: finding some need of that group which matches something those doing the ministry can give away without cost. What sorts of thing would that be? Computer knowledge, a language, knowledge of how to survive in the new country or work skills needed on a dairy farm.

As we have built our educational work since 1994, we have always kept an imaginary woman in mind. She lives in Kuala Lumpur, Malaysia. She is a Christian woman who runs a small shop. She works 60 hours every week in her four-meter by four-meter shop. She has neighbors who are recent immigrants from rural southern China. They work in lowest level jobs and have many needs. Our shopkeeper woman has a couple of friends who also want to reach out with the love and message of Jesus to these neighbors. They all work long hours, have very little money, but they are willing to spend one night a week for one school year learning the insights of Mission*Shift* Institute. In their land, a local church is able to present the whole course for only the equivalent of a couple hundred dollars per year.

Our goal is to train thousands of people like her, training tens of thousands of church members to reach out to their immigrant neighbors. Every city in the world is filling with people of other cultures. Reaching them with the holistic Gospel of Jesus will be the great challenge and opportunity of the global church for the 21st Century!

OK, those are our presuppositions, now let's get back to learning a specific cultural people-group.

A Simple Four-Step Method for Reaching an Unreached People Group

The key for effective outreach is to do your homework first! That was the most important sentence in this book; if you do not remember anything else in this book, memorize that sentence! Since 1995, students of Mission*Shift* Institute (MSI) have used the following four sets of questions to do their homework, to learn about a people group and begin a simple outreach. In MSI, we cover this in 16 weeks, from the introduction of the project to their final report. We break the class into four-person teams. We ask the students to spend a *maximum* of one hour per week in researching. For them this is a large class project; even so, students, their churches or other ministries interested in reaching the same group have gone on to build on several of these projects.

Of course, if one were interested in building such a ministry to a group near them, they could spend as much time as they wished, but consistent with our model, excellent ministries have been built with only a few hours of involvement per week. Time-wise, three fourths of our process is research. The entire process needs to be bathed in prayer. In class, it may be just an assignment, but the Holy Spirit keeps showing up and bringing people together around these plans.

The first step is to do as much "book-learnin'" research as possible about the people group and its history, using the Internet and library. The data is gathered and team members share this with each other.

The second step is to take that information, and use it as the basis of learning more from local folks who have worked with the immigrant group. This information is gleaned from interviews with social agencies, schools, law enforcement, real estate agents, store owners, etc.

The third step is now to go out and meet members of the target group, beginning to build relationships and learn more about those particular people at that particular time. As you approach people let them know that you are interested in building a small non-profit to help their people.

Finally, the fourth step is, as the group weighs their information, finding a deep, appropriate need they can work to meet, (which is God's prepared "access point,") a plan will form.

After twenty-plus years of tweaking, here is the method we have come up with to begin a simple, holistic ministry to local unreached people groups.

Ministry Example: Mission*Shift* Institute's Unreached People Group Project:
Unreached People Group Project - Mission*Shift* Institute
Step One - Book/Internet Information - Getting the basics!

- Bathe the task in prayer; get people praying with you.
- Use the Internet! Wikipedia (may be inaccurate), CIA information website, etc.
- Library; yearly almanacs; National Geographic magazines;
- Journal and magazine articles; recent books, etc.
- Who are these people? What defines them as a group? What are the sub-groups?
- What can you learn about their country?
- Politics: Who holds power in their homeland; why? How is power shared; what is their structure; what are the revolutionary structures (if applicable); and role of armed forces?
- What's their history; tell about their recent conflict; why are they part of a group forced to move?
- Weather; climate; crops; natural resources; distribution of wealth.
- What can you learn about their culture: Religion; music; arts; architecture?
- What has been the impact of Christianity in their country?
- What image/understanding of Christianity do they have?
- What can you learn about their language; do they have a literature?
- What is distinctive about their culture? What would they be proud of? Customs? Manners?
- How did they happen to come here? What was the crisis? (learn about this in depth—this will be a part of their cultural heritage for generations) What was the route? What precipitated it? Who are the people on the move? What do they have in common? What do you see as their needs?

Step Two-
Meet the Providers - Learn what others have learned - Stand on their shoulders

By providers, we mean the non-profit organizations who brought the refugees here (in the case of refugees) school districts, police, medical clinics (hospital social workers are the best there), fire and emergency responders, real estate agents, rental agents, managers of large stores, etc. What we're looking for are people who have worked with our target group, learned about them and their struggle, and have a sense of how they are doing at this point of the acculturation curve. Our first information sources are these prime sources.

If the target group has been here for a while, they may have group-led organizations that that can offer good insights as to the needs as well, as these are their people.   This is particularly true if there is a second wave of a group.

We discourage our students from speaking at this stage to any other non-profit or church group already working with the target population, being careful not to absorb that ministry's vision, value judgments, analysis of the deepest needs, etc.   As you speak to any provider, remember their analysis may or may not be accurate. Many ministries begin their work with blind assumptions, and never do research.   That is why they fail. Gather your own data, pray and discern your own analysis.   Share it with the team.

Questions for Providers
- Bathe the task in prayer; get people praying with you. Keep them updated with what you are finding and what they need to pray for next.
- Who brought this immigrant group here? Who is working with them now? Like: Lutheran Social Services; Catholic Charities; schools; welfare system; World Relief; medical people; law enforcement people; international students; community organizations: Examples: Lao Community Organization, Centro Cultural Chicano, etc.
- 'What can you tell me about the _____?
- What is bringing them here? What is their history? (Learn more) This may contradict your other sources and

cause you to do more research. (When you consistently hear a contradiction about the people, it doesn't mean that one idea or the other is wrong; it may be both are true and this gives a clue to some key paradox in the culture.)

• What was the pattern of them coming here? What draws them to this place?

• What is the structure of the families coming here? Are they intact nuclear families? Matriarchal clusters? Singles?

• What sorts of cultural challenges have they faced? How does their culture cause them problems? What is hardest for them to 'get' in the culture here?

• What sorts of needs do they face? Jobs? Housing? Education?

• How are they relating to your organization? What has caused friction/difficulties?

• What needs of the _____ are not being met? What is the next step for them to take?

• Where are the people living? Where are they moving to next? How are the families structured? How are the family roles structured? How are the family living arrangements structured?

• Where can I meet these people? Where do they gather? Where are their stores?

Share your findings with your group.

Step Three- Meet the People Group

Note: Taking what you have learned in Steps One and Two, above, think through your game plan about what you seek to learn from the immigrant interviewees. After Step Two, you will probably need to go back to the library and Internet to answer your new questions, find more information as needed, etc.

As you speak to your interviewees, leave your questions open-ended; realize that what you have learned second-handed so far may be *inaccurate!* Have a plan, follow the sections below, but be sure to compare what the interviewees say to the "common knowledge." Do not yet jump to conclusions; be hesitant to begin direct witness or proclamation; at this point, you are *listening to them!* You are the learner, not the teacher.

You should try to have more than one session with your interviewees. This is about creating relationships.

Questions for Interviewees-

- Bathe the task in prayer; get people praying with you. Ask them to pray for your meetings with individuals, that through them God will reveal his "access point."
- Find the individuals; learn their history. Tell them you are taking a class; you would like to find out about their culture and history.
- Make sure they know you are not a police officer, ICE (immigration agents) or a reporter. Explain that carefully. It will take more than one visit.
- Ask open-ended questions; avoid anything that can be answered with 'yes' or 'no.'
- Listen for the rhythm of their speech; give them time for an answer. Listen as people of their group meet, greet and talk to get a sense of how conversation works in their culture.
- Some cultures will first give you the answer they think you will want to hear. If you pause and keep listening, you may get a second, real, answer.
- Get them to tell you their story- how did they get here? (Again, make sure they know you're not ICE if you're talking to a possible undocumented immigrant.) If they are undocumented, this question should be further down.)

Questions:

- Learn what was hard about getting here. Find out who has helped them. What has been hardest here? What has been puzzling or funny?
- Ask about their foods; their language; their traditions; their holidays; about what families do when they are having good times; share your own story when appropriate; but mostly just listen. In our culture, the more you listen, the more they will like you; I would guess that that is universal.
- Ask about their business/work. Did they do this work in their homeland? How is business different here? What is

hard about getting into business here?

- They may have much better answers the second time you meet, as they will have had time to reflect on your questions.
- What would they like to see created here to make their life easier? What would they like to be able to learn? What is most frustrating to them?
- What is their religious background? How do they practice it? What is most central? How do they gather for worship? How often? Where? How is it different here from worship at home?
- How do they understand Christianity? What is attractive in it? What is unattractive?
- What are their perceived needs? What do *you* think are their real needs?

Step Four: Finally, Build Your Plan

Note: By this point of your study, you will have a lot of information from your listening so far in this project. Now you're going to begin to prayerfully build.

Having completed your first round of research, *now* you may confer with Christian ministries or ethnic congregations in order to find out what they are now doing, BUT not to get their ideas or copy their work. You may wish to share your information together, but remember, they may not have done their homework or learned what you have learned. Don't be thrown off track because they reject or disagree with your ideas. Offer to share your research and suggestions to them when you are done.

Questions to Answer to Create Your Plan

- Bathe the task in prayer; get people praying with you. Tell them the stage you're in and ask for wisdom and insight.
- What is God's access point? This is the key concept; what particular need or situation gives the greatest opportunity for building relationships and bringing the Gospel? This is where you are heading at the bottom of this section. Hold that question in your head.
- How will that need change in the next few years as

the group becomes more acculturated?
- Will more individuals with the same need be coming in the future?
- Which need have you found that will serve as a way to reach them?
- What are their true needs?
- Where are their needs slipping through the cracks?
- How are they being misunderstood?
- How can you learn more about those needs?
- How can you test those needs, to see if they are accurate?
- What sort of ministry will meet the needs? How can you focus the ministry? How can you focus it sharper? How can you focus it even more sharply? (Get it?)
- What part of the group are you reaching? How is that part defined?
- What is your mission statement?
- How will you bring proclamation into your work?
- *Where* is the ministry needed? How long will it need to stay there? What will movement of the group do to the ministry?
- What in the Christian message will get in the way of the group?
- What is your timetable?
- What help do you need?
- To whom will you need to communicate, to reach, in the community, in local churches and parachurches, to funders, to clients, to the neighborhood, city, neighborhood leaders, sources of volunteers? How will your message need to be tailored for each group?
- Who will you turn to for partnership? For workers?
- Outline a budget, prioritize and list possible funders, if needed
- How will you re-evaluate?
- How can you best present this to others and churches you may visit?
- With whom will you need to communicate-, churches,

funders, etc.? Which media for each?

• What more do you need to learn and flesh out? Do you need displays? The media scene has changed a great deal in the past decade. Newspapers are shrinking and covering less local news. Radio stations, even Christian radio stations often depend on programing sources far away, and it's very hard to get local news on the air. Social media offer some amazing opportunities, but the preferred platform "app" seems to change weekly!

One Method to Start the Process

There are an infinite number of ways to begin a cross-cultural ministry. It is interesting that throughout the book of Acts, Paul never used the same method twice as he entered a city. The one thing we can see is that he studied the city, its people, its traditions and culture. Each time he studied carefully and observed, and only then began to reach out.

So often well-intentioned individuals enter a new ministry situation, full of excitement and good intentions, carrying with them some knowledge of how ministry has worked in a different place. If they go forward to build a ministry based on the presuppositions of the previous location, culture and situation, they will fail.

A certain megachurch in our area has built its identity on the idea that they have it all together. Over the past couple of decades, they have sent teams to urban settings to "help" those urban churches to grow, to "get it" like they have. The congregation began by supporting the urban church with a few thousand dollars per year. They sent teams, who have gone in with all kinds of great expectations and with great self-assurance that they would succeed, because they had the answers.

Each time, they have wrested control away from the people of the neighborhood church. At first, the church's old members are happy with this—the cavalry has come over the hill to save their beloved church! The old members then began to sit back, and let the newcomers go to work. A few old members floated away because of change. With all this "free" money coming in, their giving was not needed. The congregation's heroic stewardship thus fell apart. The team would take over more and more, but the team ignored the history and culture of both the congregation and the neighborhood. They had come to fix things, but they don't even understand what is broken. Each time, after a year or so, the team got frustrated because they didn't see the response they expected from the church or neighborhood. The megachurch leadership saw this as failure, and moved to cut its losses. It lessened the financial support it was giving, and the city church collapsed. The heroic historic church could have been saved, if the support had been done right, and if the newcomers would have taken time to study the situation. Now it's destroyed. That particular megachurch has done this to several struggling congregations, and still doesn't "get it." They have invented a very painful form of euthanasia ministry. District staff of denominations often follow the same course—give support, expect quick change, destroy the giving base, lose interest, and pull the plug.

Studying the setting, culture and history of a congregation and its neighborhood are critical to getting things right. Before the first program activity happens, those wishing to work with a particular immigrant group, in a particular setting need to spend hundreds of hours in study. If they do not fully understand all these things, they will fail. Not might, will.

In an urban cross-cultural setting, everything seems to take about five times longer to organize than in other settings. I have served as a successful pastor in suburban, rural, rural open country, exurban and urban settings. Because of the added complexity of the city, everything you try is much, much harder to build. The combination of complexity, multicultural challenges, spiritual forces, plus the interplay of economic, governmental policy and historical decisions creates a thick interplay of forces that invisibly affect every decision and action.

This four-part method we call the Unreached People Group Project is the best way we have found to make sure that we are not starting out in ignorance and arrogance. We begin with humility, curiosity and tenacity. We realize that to be successful, we will have to be continual learners. If not, we will fail.

So how do we train our people? How do we give them the tools they need and the basic simple understandings they need to effectively cross-cultural boundaries? God is sending everybody everywhere.   How do we teach our people to put this tripartite model to work in the midst of this worldwide diaspora?   That is our next chapter.

Chapter Six:
How Can We Train Our Church Members for the Task?

As the church begins to understand the need and immensity of the task ahead, we need to develop models to train the American and global church. Early on, I was struck by the sheer number of cross-cultural outreach attempts that failed. Earnest, joyful, Spirit-led people came to our core-city neighborhood, began cross-cultural outreaches, failed and gave up. They kept hitting invisible walls, stuff they didn't know that they didn't know or need to know. Cross-cultural outreach with immigrants is very, very hard. It takes a great deal of study of the people group, its culture, its needs, its level of acculturation in the new culture and the issues of the community around it.

Having spent thirty-some years trying learn how to train people, this chapter is about what we have learned. The way we did it is NOT the only way to train people, but by sharing what we've learned, we may give you some ideas of where you can start, helping you to stand on our shoulders. This chapter is about the kinds of things we think believers need to learn before they begin cross-cultural ministry.

I) Where do we Begin, to Train Christians in the Pew?

Throughout the history of the church, it has struggled with how to *equip the saints for the work of ministry. (Ephesians 4:12)* We can imagine that in the first three centuries of the often-persecuted church, ministry was mentored much in the way we see Paul training Barnabas or Timothy on the missionary journeys. As we look at the early church fathers, we see that letters from Christian leaders and the local congregation were used to teach new believers and developed leadership from within.

The Early Church

In the early 300s AD Roman Emperor Constantine made Christianity legal; the first church councils like Nicea soon followed, and the church began rapid growth. It became a much more public and visible institution, with larger and larger buildings. The bishops of the larger cities grew in importance, and these churches became the center of a more formalized type of training for leaders. It seems to have had a very strong component of learning by doing, all in the busy life of the urban center. The church began to lift up the spiritual gift of pastor as the normative leadership of the church, which evolved into a dichotomy of lay-clergy which remains dominant today.

Monasticism

With the rise of monasticism in the fifth and sixth centuries, the ideal became to disengage from the city, even to the extent of the desert hermits. The monastery, away from the city, its connectedness and the demands of secular life became the center of Christian learning. Ironically, in a world today where about sixty-five percent of all people live in cities, we still train our pastors in settings and by methods that discourage engagement with the city!

The University

As universities arose in the twelfth century, they became the model of training the professional theologian. Clergy became highly trained, literate, sometimes even adding Greek and Hebrew to the standard Latin of the west. The laity remained generally illiterate; worship centered on monastic choirs while lay people stood or milled about. The pilgrimage and the pilgrimage-centered medieval church with ornate stained-glass windows became the high-tech medium teaching Bible stories and other Christian content to the fortunate laity who could afford to take leave of their work for the holy touristing of the pilgrimage.

The Reformation

Before the time of the Reformation in the 16th Century, most European lay Christians remained illiterate. Preaching was a very small part of the mass, and teaching was rare for most lay Christians. Superstition and the self-serving churchly teachings such as Purgatory served mainly as a stewardship method.

The Reformation was highly dependent on the concurrent invention of the movable-type printing press. Gutenberg's press became the printer's angel to spread Luther and Calvin's pamphlets far and wide. A newly-literate laity could afford few books, but the penny tract became a powerful and popular tool. Luther decried the ignorance of his people, and sought to train them through translating Scripture into their language, publishing his Large and Small Catechisms. Reformed and Lutheran sermons were strong on teaching both Scripture and theology. Even so, the University remained the central means of training the professional leadership to a level far beyond that of the lay member.

Today's Feudal Church

In the medieval period, Europe saw the rise of feudalism. It was a type of governance and civil structure with a "lord" who was the most powerful hereditary landowner in a given area and his vassal peasants who were linked to him by promises of fealty. They were bound by oath to spend a certain part of their time working on the lord's estate. We think of feudalism as being ancient, but as we look at structures like officer-enlisted, management-labor, and clergy-lay we can see that this lord-peasant structure has very real echoes being lived out daily in our lives. Are we really willing to be medieval peasants in the church in the Twenty-first Century? Is this the biblical model, or like the old joke, are clergy paid to be good, whereas lay members are good for nothing?

The 20th Century American peacetime draft had one other effect on the church. To stay out of the draft, students had to attend an *accredited* school. This had the effect of standardizing secondary education, and killed off many informal Bible schools that had been such a large part of the lay life in the early 20th Century. Many denominations had to develop more formal seminaries, with professors who were forced into the norms of academia in order to have adequate credentials to teach at these accredited schools. Ecclesiastical feudalism became more entrenched.

21st Century Education– Exploding Possibilities

As we enter the 21st Century, suddenly all of these forms are being shaken up, torn down and rethought. Who would have ever guessed that Microsoft would become one of the major educators? A student can spend a few thousand dollars and a few months to earn Microsoft certifications, and step directly into a good-paying job, one that pays more than the student who went through eight years of college and seminary—and ended up with $75,000 in debt! That same seminarian was taught many important scholarly disciplines, but learned virtually nothing about practical ministry and nothing about cross-cultural outreach to the 75 million immigrants in our midst.

Today with TED talks, thousands of courses on iTunes U, Massive Open Online Courses (MOOCs) offered by universities all over the globe, online courses at every college, endless information on the Internet, and the pandemic-caused explosion of distance learning, suddenly the world of education has radically changed. What global higher education will like by 2050 is the source of endless hours of speculation among academics and students today. Dozens of new paradigms are being tested. Time will tell.

The bottom line for the church is that the pastor is now just one more person with a Master's degree, and lay people are hungry to learn. Lay people want to enter, develop and succeed in ministry to a degree never seen in the history of Christianity. Today we have tools that make it possible that a class in Minneapolis can talk face-to-face in real time with a missionary in Kiev, Mombasa or Quito. These courses can be structured in a myriad of ways, and any level, use resources from all over the globe, many learning methods, and be tailored to fit any age or need—all right in the congregation! Smartphone apps will soon be available to translate a language in real time, so a course could simultaneously be given in an interactive format with people all over the globe.

II) What We Discovered Our Task to Be

In our decades of attempting to equip the church, we discovered that the task is made up of several parts. One is that we need to change the religious consumer in the pew into a front-line missionary. At a time when the American church is collapsing, its future is going to be decided by how well we equip and send the next generation. But we do not need to train them as clergy. We need to take them, trained as they are, engaged in their current workplace, shopping in their normal stores, sleeping on their own pillows, living as a regular neighbor—and turn them loose to be front-line missionaries. We have to change their self-awareness, their expectation, their identity, their sense of call, and give them permission to become church builders. We need to find a way to get past our feudal dependence and orientation on pastors, and equip the saints for the work of ministry.

We need to do this by teaching people to develop bite-sized or "hobby" ministries. All sorts of people enjoy golf, skiing, swimming or tennis without becoming professionals. Why do we demand that in the church? It's interesting to see how things work in the Yoiddo Full-Gospel Church in Seoul, South Korea I mentioned earlier. It's a congregation of over 800,000 members, all based on lay-led house churches. As soon as a person comes to faith, they immediately involve that person in ministry and witness a few hours each week. That's how they learn.

In chapter five, I mentioned our imaginary student in Kuala Lumpur. We want to produce millions of believers like her all over the world. We don't need even an undergraduate degree. We just need to give people basic training, change their self-concept from church consumer to producer, teach them how to learn and give them permission with support.

We need to change our expectation of what a church member is. We can end church feudalism in our time! After a generation of seeker-friendly, least-common denominator, mile-wide but inch-deep, no cross, consumer-Christianity we are seeing the Millennial generation turn away in droves. The Walmarting of the American church has nearly destroyed it. Now it is time to grasp our young people with the passion to creatively love, serve and witness to their immigrant neighbor. It's the only way we will have a multicultural American church in a couple generations.   Jesus is the only one who can unify us for the task ahead, which is the re-evangelization of North America and Europe.

Bite-Sized Ministries That Fit Our Lives

Reaching out to our neighbor does not take money or thousands of hours of time. A few years ago, one of our Unreached People Group teams chose the large community of Chinese students at the University of Minnesota.   The team discovered that here on the northern tundra, somehow it has developed that our university has more high level doctoral, post-doc and guest lecturer students than any other university in the US.   These are people, who when they return to lead China, would be at such a high social level that none of us mere mortals would ever be able to approach or get to know them.

They learned that about 80 percent of these Chinese future leaders are never invited into an American home!   Most of these students read and write English very well, but have had little chance to practice simple conversational English.   They are very eager to learn to speak English well, and to make American friends.   The team did several hours of study, first learning about the history and culture of this group.   Then they went to meet others who are working with this group.   They learned that four Christian ministries were already offering conversational English to these Chinese, but they kept digging.   They particularly liked the balance and discipling of one of the groups.   As they approached the leaders of this ministry, they mentioned they could do so much more if they had a few more volunteers.

A couple members of our team had just graduated from one of our local Christian universities, so they then went back to their college to see how the school could plug in.   The director of the college's ESL program was delighted to hear about their research. She said that one of their greatest needs was finding a place for their students to plug in and practice.   Bingo.

At the end of the semester, the team gave their 60-some slide PowerPoint presentation, outlining the history, culture and worldview of the Chinese students.   They explained what they had found.   They mentioned what the Chinese students and providers had mentioned. Finally, they presented their vision. They said that to reach these high-ranking Chinese students, they needed several things:

1) A person who owned a computer,
2) Who had Internet access,
3) Who had an email account,
4) Who had one hour available each week to arrange rides for the students of the Christian college to come to the University-neighborhood church to volunteer in the ESL program.

That was it. One hour a week. A computer, Internet and email. That was all that stood in the way of introducing these Christ-hungry, English-hungry brilliant young leaders to Christ.

That's a well-researched, focused, Spirit-led mini-ministry that could touch hundreds of lives, without leaving your kitchen! Do you have an hour per week? If you find God's access point, that may be all you need.

What we need to teach our people is to open their eyes, their hearts and their mouths. We need to turn them around in the pews, and see that their calling is "out there." Because "out there" is now right here.

III) The Mission*Shift* Vision
As a Christian pastor, educator or lay leader, what do you need to study to attempt the task? Here is the vision:

The Challenge:
In 1800, only 2.5% of the world's population lived in cities. In 1900, it had grown to 10%. Today, half of the world's population lives in vast metro areas. By 2050, 75%!

At the same time, we're in the midst of the greatest human migration in history; perhaps two billion people are on the move inside or outside their home country. Thus, every exploding global city is a home to many cultures. *How will we reach them with the Gospel?*

The Universal Needs of the City
Cities worldwide share the same problems: isolated nuclear families; poverty; chemical dependency; sex trafficking; mental

illness; housing and development issues; gangs; justice and prison systems; prostitution; HIV/AIDS and much more. *These swirling, teeming diaspora cities are multi-cultural, and each sub-group requires a meaningful approach with the Gospel within their own cultural milieu, in the midst of their own needs.* To serve in the city, we need an understanding of what makes up a culture and how to cross cultural boundaries. We need to understand other world cultures, world religions and how to recognize access points for the Gospel.

We, as the church, have never faced a situation like this. The book needs to be re-written. Our American cities will be reached only in the same way. We need to teach hundreds of thousands of entrepreneurial leaders to build the urban church here and worldwide!

The Tri-Partite Model

The central task of the church is proclaiming the Gospel and making disciples of Jesus Christ; however, this doesn't exist in a vacuum, it happens in a world of profound human need. The Gospel is most fully shared in the midst of these needs by building relationships. Where these three parts intersect, Gospel Proclamation-Need-

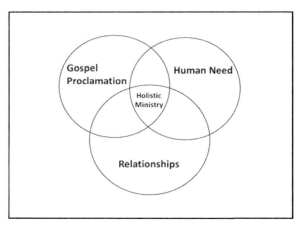

Relationship, that is holistic ministry. Whenever the church rediscovers this, it thrives, whether we look at Jesus, Hudson Taylor, Wesley, Francke, Hauge or Yongii Cho.

The Local City as a Laboratory

We have used south Minneapolis as our learning lab. Minnesota, because of our rich tradition of refugee resettlement, is unique. Here we are, a Midwestern metro area of four million people, landlocked in the center of the continent, with great supporting human services, and now our city is filled with people from all over the world. The pattern is not unique, but the level of diversity is. Our church found it was in the midst of over 100 distinct people groups! We had here a God-given laboratory, with all of the educational riches of our metro area, with committed Christians all around us, with the ability to train believers to reach almost any culture on earth! That determined our vision and call.

Local mission is now global; global mission (and all mission) is local; thus, all ministry today is *glocal.* We need to study and deeply learn our neighborhoods, their people-groups and their needs in order to serve effectively. At the same time, each neighborhood is changing in hundreds of ways. Property values are going up or down. Groups of people are moving in or out. Resources are flowing in or out, etc. Economic swings constantly change the picture. *We need to build ministry to meet what is coming, not what is.* To do that, we have to intimately know and understand the area in which we work, so we can anticipate who will be our neighbors.

Together We Have Many Strengths

Our congregation had a history of being a catalyst to bring people together in ministry. We brought this history, along with our knowledge of the city, our program, an ability to organize and teach, and our facilities. You have many tools available as well: your building, your neighboring churches, your denomination, local social service providers, Universities, ethnic leaders, real estate people who know who's moving in and out, local schools who are way ahead of you in knowing who your

> *Use the leaders of the city to teach the city to the people of the city.*

newcomers are, politicians, governmental workers, and many more. All of these are resources that you can call on to teach you how to reach those around you. *YOU personally don't need to know everything- but you're surrounded by people who know particular areas very well- and they can teach you and your people what they need to know.* We learned to pair city and suburb with the educational resources around us. *Use the leaders of the city, to teach the city, to the people of the city!* Like the old children's story of "The Stone Soup," if we each bring a bit of what we have, together we can share quite a feast!

Contextual

Understanding the nuances of a given neighborhood is a key to success in cross-cultural ministry. This means understanding the history, function, governmental, economic, racial, cultural, financial, religious, legal and relational identity of your neighborhood. To do cross-cultural outreach, a student must understand the city from a neighborhood level. Further, this knowledge must be multi-dimensional with a good understanding of the inter-relatedness of all these functions. We teach the students how to go home and study their own neighborhood.

Entrepreneurial

To do cross-cultural ministry means to become an entrepreneur. A key expertise is learning to start on bare ground and build a simple ministry. This key skill, of starting with no money, learning to share a vision and gather resources is central to the future of diaspora ministry.

Missiological

Christians, to be effective, need to approach cross-cultural ministry from a missiological standpoint. It is not a continuation of mid-20th century urban ministry paradigms. It presents a great deal of information on urban problems and people-care, but the focus is on bringing people to a personal encounter with Jesus Christ. We believe that Jesus Christ is the most important resource for immigrant people. We also believe that the strange 20th century American split between "social gospel" and "evangelical gospel" is unbiblical and a false dichotomy. Jesus reached out to the whole person, and both aspects of ministry belong to the Church; this is holistic ministry. One cannot exist without the other.

Training Needs a Simple Beginning

We found it was important give students just enough training so they would feel confident beginning or assisting in an urban, or diaspora or immigrant non-profit ministry. They need "Diaspora 101," providing information, but more importantly, a conceptual framework on which to build additional training. For example, two hours of training in chemical dependency is not enough to do chemical dependency ministry; but if the student has had no background in the area, knowing the significance of AA, the disease model, the twelve-step program, family systems theory and intervention will provide the tools to continue study. It also gives them the resources necessary to see chemical dependency as a root cause of urban problems and where to go to get help for a chemically dependent person.

Dawning Technology

Using the best of modern technology, we want to re-discover the training methods of the fourth century—training people experientially in a given area. Lectures/presentations can be recorded and shared globally at no cost. Experts on the other side of the country or globe are a couple of clicks away. Figure out what your people need to learn, and you'll find the resources are already out there. Internet technology is developing at a breath-taking rate, which will allow students globally to access what we've learned, and teach us what they've found that works.

Training Your People Inter-connects a City

Through our educational networking, a rich network of congregations, ministries, schools, practitioners and ethnic leaders was developed. Students met the practitioners and experience this networking. Each of the entities is enriched by the interaction. Suburban churches develop contacts in the city. Students plug into existing ministries. Ethnic leaders get new contacts with students, their churches, their colleges, etc. From these students you train, your church and local non-profits will find a source of eager, trained volunteers or staffers.

Our Graduates Create New Ministries

We found that students, once trained in each area, benefitted from what we called the "Unreached People Group Project." By the end of the year, was a part of a team that developed a very specific plan to reach an unreached people group in the area. Several of those plans have become working ministries, and several more are being used by specialized ministries to expand their work.

Training "Just Regular" Christians is Life-Changing

The most surprising outcome of being trained is how it changed the lives of the students. Many said that it was the most exciting, compelling training they have taken. Seminary students say that it is the most practical course they have experienced.

Summary

What we have found is that all these pieces create a four-way interaction. We thought we started out to transfer **cognitive information**. We had learned stuff, and we wanted to give it to them. That certainly happens, but there is much more.

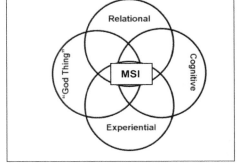

Throughout training, **relationships** form between students, presenters, ethnic leaders, teacher, colleges, congregations, neighborhood leaders. All of these work together to enrich the experience.

Training is enhanced by the **experiential** aspect. Get your people out into your neighborhood. Students should have assignments that bring them into interaction with the people of the neighborhood. Training needs to be strong on experiences, with exciting teachers and meaty presentations on interesting topics outside their comfort zone, games and more.

Finally, we found that many of our students experience a profound deepening of their faith and sense of call. The Holy Spirit shows up as God's Word is laid out, as people share their stories and the reality of Jesus in speakers' lives shines out. For lack of a better term, with a bit of a smile, we just call that the **God Thing**.

Training to see and understand these new dimensions of students' faith lives profoundly changes their identity and sense of call. In a qualitative study we did, this change in identity was a very strong outcome in the class for many of its students, and led to a new sense of call, new areas of individual outreach and many new involvements in diaspora ministry.[12]

V) What Are the Areas We Need to Learn?

Over the past twenty-five years, we found there were seven distinct areas of study needed:

1) The City-- Learning About the City and How it Works

This includes getting to know the designated laboratory neighborhood—its history, geography, trends, people groups, business structure, ownership patterns, recreation patterns, demographics, assets, money flow, resources, leaders and more. Good general readings are

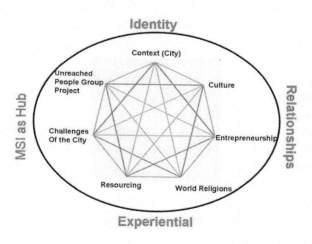

important, but equally important are the experiential, confidence-building field trips and other exercises that get the student out, learning to meet the people.

2) Culture & How to Cross Cultural Boundaries

Culture is a new concept to many people, so it's important to spend a good deal of time considering this topic. Central to the learning are a couple of great texts: Paul Sparks and Tim Soerens, *The New Parish: How Neighborhood Churches Are Transforming Mission, Discipleship and Community* and Patty Lane's *A Beginner's Guide to Crossing Cultures*. We also use readings by people including missiologists like Ralph Winter and his seminal article, written for Lausanne '74: *The New Macedonia: A Revolutionary New Era in Mission Begins*.[13] Field trips and individual assignments that create cross-cultural experiences are helpful. We look at what it means to cross these boundaries by watching the old film *Hudson Taylor.* We bring in guest speakers who are individuals from our culture who have served abroad; we have speakers from other cultures who have come here.

3) "Entrepreneuring" the Church

We developed a six-hour course on how does one begin a ministry. This section taught people how to step into a situation, analyze it, and begin to build a cross-cultural ministry, with no money! It begins with the six-hour course, is revisited in visits for analysis of a non-profit, and is brought to fullness in the final unit, where students create a plan to reach an unreached people group. This "mini-MBA" teaching looks at the biblical presuppositions on discerning and building a ministry, the role of the leader, and a theology of resourcing.

4) World Religions

We found that a simple introduction into the major world religions was important for people to have. Today, as never before, we are surrounded by people of many other world religions and concepts of reality. Simple presentations on the major world religions, combined with Halverson's *The Compact Guide to World Religions,* or Morgan's *Understanding World Religions in 15 Minutes a Day* give a good overview of the world's major religions and their access points for Christian witness.

5) Resourcing

Most lay folks have never taken the time to figure out how to fund simple ministry. If we can figure out how to do it without money, that's ideal. God provides. Some simple teaching, from a theology of abundance, students need to look at approaches to communication, vision casting, and fundraising.

6) Challenges of the City

As your people begin to do ministry with immigrants, they need to learn how to begin ministry to people who are in need. Poverty, culture shock, Post-Traumatic Stress Disorder (PTSD), chemical dependency, mental illness, immigration law, kids and gangs and even how local governmental structures work and much more complicate the immigrant's entry to their new country. We found we needed to give some background in these areas. *We used the leaders of the city to teach the city to the people of the city.* Two hours on chemical dependency doesn't equip students to be CD counselors, but it does teach some resources, like what is AA, what is a 12-step program, big book, Al-Anon, etc.

7) The Unreached People Group Project

This is the capstone project for the course, where students, in small groups, create a plan combining human need, relationships and proclamation of the Gospel. Using the four-part sequence explained in chapter five, they study the people group, talk to service providers, meet the people group and make a plan. Many of these become functioning mini-ministries. Start on bare dirt, with no money, and build!

Chapter Seven:
What is the Best Model for Assisting the Growth of a Church for Immigrants?
A History of Failure

Across America, for a couple of generations, existing congregations have attempted to welcome non-English speaking immigrants, with very little success. As we said in chapter two, when I challenged you to join the Korean-language church in your neighborhood, immigrants coming to your church face huge obstacles in becoming a part of your fellowship. The obstacles of language and culture are barriers to developing intimacy and friendship, which is central to becoming part of a church. Is it possible to change an existing church into a multicultural church?

Another area of huge controversy regarding immigrants is whether we should be building multicultural churches or language- and culture-specific churches to reach them. We'll work on that in this chapter as well. As we look at bringing immigrant people into the Body of Christ, what is the best way? In the end, there is no best way. The "best way" depends on many things, which we will think through in this chapter.

Monocultural Church Plants for the First Generation

As wave after wave of European immigrants came to North America from sixteenth through nineteenth centuries, they brought their own form of Christianity with them. These were specialized by language, region, doctrine and even the particular revival current in their home country. Because that revival was often a reaction to the last move of the Spirit, perhaps a century before, when they came to America and found those who were doggedly faithful to the former revival; that too caused a separation. The descendants of each wave continued to carry on the emphases of what was going on in the homeland church at the time they emigrated. If they continued to speak their mother tongue, they continued the same old-fashioned speech, long after the language had morphed in their home countries. In the same way, they carried those theological tendencies as being best for the church, which later spawned church associations, denominations and synods.

In each home country, as the pendulum of church emphasis gradually oscillated between head and heart, faith and works, ecumenical openness or distrust, outreach or inreach, each immigrant wave differed in their vision of the church. For example, among German Lutherans, each successive wave found itself uncomfortable with the German Lutherans they found already here. They had been influenced by the direction of the church they left behind, which had reacted to the direction of the earlier generation(s). The pendulum had swung, but the Germans they found in the new land had not been a part of that pendulum swing. Some of the sensed distance may have also been due to the higher level of assimilation the earlier group had reached. Finally, these Germans who were already here were like older siblings, same but different. Who would it be most natural for the newcomers to define themselves over against but their nearest siblings?

I am an only child, and it fascinates me how my friends gain such a sense of their identity from how different they are from their siblings. Couldn't you explain for several hours how you're different from your siblings? Yet, to me, you and your siblings would seem remarkably the same. For immigrants, the beliefs and forms of those who proceeded them became either something to adopt, or more likely, something to reject, all for the sake of *identity*.

For immigrants, the church often became the one place of feeling safe in the midst of an alien country. After several generations, that church culture in the new land, even though it might have changed a great deal from their grandparents' church, became the "right" church culture. Even in small towns, there was often an Irish Catholic church just down the block from the German Catholic church; both spoke English, but each lived on with their hyphenated nationality, for the sake of *identity*. In Chicago, Serbs and Croats continued to live out their cultures and historic differences in their respective Serbian Orthodox and Roman Catholic churches, even though they spoke the same Serbo-Croatian language.

The church and the home language often hung on for a remarkable length of time in these enclaves. My father-in-law was born in 1929 in rural Carver County, Minnesota. The towns in that county form a very German community where business on Main Street was still being done in German into the 1970s. He was born in the United States. His parents were born in here. His grandparents were born in this country. His great-grandparents came to Carver County in 1865. He was the third generation born on this soil, but when he began school in 1935, he couldn't speak a single word of English! Even through World War One, they had clung to their heritage. It wasn't until the social pressure of WWII, that the community began to function in English, more than four generations later.

All across America, the power of immigrant cultures has continued to influence the American church, as Italians, Poles, Scandinavians, Yugoslavians, various eastern Europeans, Germans and many other groups came to the United States through the beginnings of the Twentieth Century. Then, for about 50 years immigration to this country slowed to a trickle.

A Sea Change in Immigration Policy Started It All

That ended when in 1965 President Lyndon B. Johnson quietly signed a law changing US immigration policies. He said, "This bill that we will sign today is not a revolutionary bill. It does not affect the lives of millions," Johnson said at the signing ceremony. "It will not reshape the structure of our daily lives or add importantly to either our wealth or our power."[14] Little did they know! In the midst of the Vietnam War, the Great Society programs, the moon-landing program, and the building of the interstate highways, it seemed a very small thing to end quotas favoring western Europeans for immigration. Yearly, one million legal immigrants from all over the world win the State Department lottery to gain a "green card" and gain resident status in the US. The resulting change has been immense.

Preparing to Nurture Immigrant Churches

As I said in Chapters One and Two, I believe we will see another large wave of immigration through the 2030s. With perhaps 75 million immigrants and their families here, and another large wave on the way, now is the time for the American church to begin to learn to plant new immigrant churches. But how?

Having looked at the acculturation curves in chapter two, we saw that only a tiny part of each immigrant group are early adopters, cultural chameleons with the desire, education and ego strength to want to fully join an existing English language congregation. Even if they find themselves warmly received, even if they gain deep friendships and have excellent English language skills, they will always, to some degree, still feel as outsiders. They will always find themselves guessing at cultural norms. They will always wonder at small things they didn't understand, laughing at puns and colloquial jokes that leave them confused, feeling a little awkward in social settings, and always learning about "that's what people do." Even if they work very well as professionals, working closely with people of the majority or other cultures, even if they seem to move effortlessly in their new culture, they will still have the most comfort in their heart language, have the closest relationships with family and friends who understand that culture, and only fully unwind when in that setting. And those are the early-adopters.

Historical Precedent Abounds

We can see, that just as most European immigrants found shelter and reluctance to change in their churches, that same pattern is being acted out now by immigrants who come here and bring or meet Jesus. My Norwegian-heritage congregation took two generations to get into English, and three to get out of Norwegian. Three! When I speak with immigrant-language church pastors around the US, they all say the same thing. Their people gather in their home language, because it is the one hour each week they can let down all their defenses, have no need for language or cultural translation, and speak heart-to-heart, faith-to-faith.

The draw may be even deeper than that. In our "American" culture, the family is a weakened institution. Individuals make decisions, move across the country, and pursue their lives with little thought as to their family's attitudes or desires. That is a very rare idea of family, globally. In most countries, the desires, values and needs of the family far overshadow the wants of the individual. Most humans gain their greatest sense of who they are from their family. For many immigrants, their church serves as a new family, giving identity and guidance.

For example, for many Mexican people coming to the US, their greatest loss is the presence of their extended family. With the advent of cheap phone cards and the spread of mobile phone technology in Latin America, many Mexican immigrants speak with their family "at home" daily. For these folks, and for many whose need for family bonds is so powerful, the immigrant church functions as a second family. Many Latino pastors actively seek to structure their congregation and its activities to fit that pattern. Most Anglos couldn't imagine celebrating Christmas or Easter all day at church, but for many immigrants, that provides them with the family experience they long for on those potentially lonely days!

Just as Americans choose their churches according to micro-cultural differences, immigrants experience the same. For example, many Latino churches will have members from several countries, but in often there will be a core of folks, who end up in leadership, who are from the same micro-culture based on the same home area. Other factors such as educational level, social standing at home, family "name," heritage, physical features, even legal status in the US may separate members of a congregation, or even be a leading commonality of a given congregation. In American existing congregations, we have white collar and blue-collar congregations too, right? Ah, that pesky homogenous unit principle.

Thus, as we help to build the immigrant church, we are wise if we learn to watch for these natural boundaries and tendencies. Bringing folks together, in their heart language, in a culturally homogenous group is the most natural way to build the immigrant church.

A Holistic Approach that Works

An example of a program that has made great strides in this area is LINC-Houston. LINC (Lutheran Inter-city Network Coalition) is a 501c3 non-profit focused on holistically planting immigrant congregations. Since 2002, backed by a group of local congregations, their method is to receive from their denomination a decommissioned church building in a first-ring suburb of Houston. These are the areas in which many of Houston's new immigrants live.

At those locations, LINC creates some services which are deeply needed by the community, such as a food shelf, clothes closet, English classes, etc. As immigrants come with their needs, LINC tracks which groups are coming to them. Next, they find some Christian, a missionary, Christian businessperson, someone who speaks that language and begins to visit these newcomers and build them into a cell group house church.

As the group comes together, the next step is critical. The group selects its own leader, who is then given a more extensive theological education by extension over the next few years. This tent-building lay pastor gradually builds the church, which as it grows, moves into sharing the worship space available at the church. Several "incubating" groups can share the building on any given weekend, with smaller groups continuing to meet in homes. Gradually the group is able to support the newly trained pastor and church. When the immigrant church gets large enough to take over its own building, the church is given another vacant church building. These buildings are repaired before giving them to the new church, so they don't inherit overwhelming deferred maintenance.

The new church then also becomes a shared ministry incubator.

Visionary founder of the program, Rev. Mark Junkans and his staff encourage each of these churches to develop their own strong leadership from the beginning, so they are not dependent on an existing congregation. Through this visionary, holistic program they have planted a couple dozen congregations in the past decade.

Beyond this, holistic ministry can take another direction. As I mentioned in the beginning, a danger in dealing with the needs of people is causing dependency. In his amazing book, *Toxic Charity: How Churches and Charities Hurt Those They Help, And How to Reverse It*, Robert Lupton makes some bold and sensible points about the destructive nature of how we have focused our charity on giving things away. Indeed, sometimes people need a bowl of soup, a safe place to sleep or *pro bono* legal help. However, we have created a system that continues to provide for people for decades, developing a level of helpless dependency that destroys the urban underclass.

The next step in holistic ministry may be away from dealing with specific needs, with people who have moved forward in the acculturation curve, moving toward people learning how they can be empowered and serve their own community. This is to move away from seeing immigrant neighbors as being people to be helped and pitied, and toward listening and recognizing their gifts so they can move from the position of taker to giver. This "asset-based community development" model can help churches move away from endless, dependency-building caregiving to empowerment and hope.

The Challenge of the Second Generation A universal challenge for the immigrant church is teaching its young. The parents are fluent in their heart language, their children in English. The parents do not feel they are fluent enough in English to teach their children, and may actually be embarrassed to teach in English because their children speak it with more fluency. Further, if the immigrants are first-generation Christian converts, they may have never been to a Sunday School class and feel daunted by the task. They

> **Sidebar:**
> **Immigrant Generation Definitions**
>
> **First Generation**- Adults who came as immigrants
>
> **1.5 Generation**- Children who were born overseas, but grew up in the new country. Those who came after about four years of age will probably speak their new language with an accent.
>
> **Second Generation**- Children of the first generation, born in the new country.

may come from an educational system that teaches children in a far different way, than the glossy workbooks, colorful art projects and the asking of open-ended questions. They may come from a culture where the teachers in their schools wrote long passages on the board, and the children copied them on their slates. This kind of rote learning is unknown in America, but the norm in many cultures. Finally, the behavior of the other Americanized students may even be a bit disrespectful which is not acceptable to parents who are trying hard to accomplish a task very new to them.

How can they get past this critical hurdle? First, training is crucial. Most communities have educators at local Christian colleges or large congregations who can help the immigrant parents. In fact, the teachers may be doing a wonderful job, but have no way to know. For a second option, a congregation may be able to enlist some volunteers from a partner congregation or from a local Christian college. A third way would be to develop a more formal partnership with an existing congregation, perhaps the one whose building they share, and join the two Sunday Schools. Team teaching may be a possibility. Perhaps at the end of the first generation, as the youngsters become the leaders of the congregation, the two churches will fully become one. For many struggling urban congregations, this may be the answer to their prayers! It will take a tremendous amount of hard work to develop that level of intimacy and trust, but there is hardly a more rewarding opportunity in the life of the American church.

How Can an Existing Church Best Help Nurture an Immigrant Church?

Our congregation has now helped to mentor seven specialized baby congregations. These relationships have been some of the greatest, most treasured experiences of my years of ministry. Our large stone building has all kinds of room; we see it as a mustard tree that can give shelter to many baby birds. We are blessed, that since 1872, we have never built our own building; we have always bought a used church and made it our home. For the past 50-some years our home has been a magnificent granite building with all kinds of great space. Because we didn't build it, our people have a peculiar freedom to share it, because we think of ourselves as stewards of the building at this time. We have learned many things, made many mistakes, and have laughed, eaten, talked and cried together for 30 years. Here are some key insights:

A) Come Alongside, Don't Control

With each group, we have had a different kind of relationship, based on their need, their desire, their culture, their maturity and their formal structure. With some groups, they just used the space for a while, and then moved off to their own building when they had grown enough. With other groups, it was their desire to work more closely with us, and so we have shared ministry and worship opportunities. We let the individual group decide what will work best for them. If we try to control the process, ignore cultural norms and particularly, if we do not respect them, it cannot go well. In an earlier chapter I talked about the megachurch that had a track record of destroying urban churches they cluelessly tried to "help." Existing churches with a paternalistic attitude fail miserably in these partnerships, because the relationship is toxic at best, racist at worst.

B) Train Your Congregation

A critical transition happened when we began to train our entire congregation to think cross-culturally. Even though our congregation has been passionately involved in world missions for more than a century, as in many American churches, the desire to support cross-cultural mission was directly proportional to the distance involved. In other words, the mission field is "out there, over there," not *my* neighbor. "I'll be happy to pray for the missionaries, but don't expect me to be involved in my own city!" That began to change as we started teaching our people. Today "out there" is now right here. For our congregation, even though they had had evangelism training in half a dozen various programs, from Evangelism Explosion to Campus Crusade and more, cross-cultural witness seemed daunting.

In 2003, from Labor Day until Christmas, our entire adult Sunday School read and discussed Patty Lane's amazing book, *"A Beginner's Guide to Crossing Cultures."*[15] Together, the group carefully studied the book, learning about this concept of *culture*. A breakthrough came when Kenny Chelmen, one of our WWII vets, raised his hand. He addressed the group something like this,

> *"When we came into North Africa in '42, they gave us mimeographed sheets about how to understand the locals. They taught us about how to greet them, what to say and not to say, and how to keep out of trouble. Each time we went to a new place, they gave us new sheets, because the customs were different in Crete, Sardinia, Italy and France. Pastor, that was about* culture, *wasn't it?"*

When he said that, there was a palpable "click" in the room. This beloved leader had validated the idea of *culture* for all of our members. It was no longer something strange and new-fangled. He opened the door for our people to fully understand and embrace the concept that these immigrants understood the world differently than us. The entire class seemed to have a new impetus to learn all these new concepts Patty Lane laid out. The class dove into the material with even more interest. We learned about differing senses of time, different senses of ownership and sharing, we learned about differing ways respect is shown and much more. Patty's book is awesome! Just as importantly, we learned *we* had a culture as well.

Our third- and fourth-generation Scandinavian-Americans still have distinct cultural traits; one of which is when talking to someone, they tend to stand three to six inches farther from the person than many Americans would. They also are uncomfortable facing the person directly; they tend to open the stance 20-30 degrees, because that's less confrontational. Confrontation is a very, very uncomfortable experience for Scandinavian-Americans.

They chuckled when they realized this, because every Sunday as our people were leaving the Sanctuary, our Latino friends would be coming for worship, so conversations would begin. For the Latinos, talking to someone meant being a few inches closer, and squarely in front of the other person. Each Sunday, as these conversations were happening, the Latinos would sense that they needed to move in closer, while the Scandinavian-Americans would sense that they needed to open up the space. Like a slow-motion waltz, gradually each of these happily conversing couples would slowly waltz around our lobby area, with neither fully understanding
what they were doing!

After completing the Lane book, we next found a little book on Latino, particularly Mexican culture, *Harvest Waiting: Reaching Out to the Mexicans.* [16] We worked our way through that. Our congregation heard about the importance of family in Mexican culture and somebody said, "Oh, that's really good!" They learned about holidays, family roles, traditions and more. Occasionally someone would be heard to say, "So that's why they do that!" Meanwhile, our Latino pastor addressed these issues with his congregation. That one six-month period changed our congregation's awareness and identity forever. As little friction points and cultural misunderstandings inevitably arose over the years, that short bit of training has brought us through time after time. Our people learned to pause and think through what was going on culturally; they learned to have patience and see things from another's perspective, and above all else to talk things through. Train your people!

C) Keep Communication Open

Another key factor of the successful sharing of a building is the necessity of spending time together and talking. In most cultures that's a normal part of friendship, not just when you need to transmit information! Making sure to find time to have an occasional lunch together, making sure to do some things together, making sure to really know how each other's families are doing, etc. is what it takes to keep that relationship going. Our American obsession with and commodification of time powerfully work against cross-cultural effectiveness. Even though I am fairly fluent in Spanish, I still make lots of gaffes, sometimes to the delight of my listening friends. In one sermon, I simple translated the English terms "spending time" and "saving time." Afterward my dear and wise friend, Pastor Joel Ramirez commented that neither of those phrases exist in Spanish. They neither spend nor save time. They simply live in it. That was a wise observation, and once again taught me that I am culturally ignorant in so many ways, even after 50 years of learning the language. It also taught me that my cultural understanding of time is not the only one; right there was a major new understanding of a different worldview. This was in communication with a culture very, very close to ours. Imagine all there is to learn about more distant cultures!

Minor conflict is sure to arise from time to time. Messes will happen. A toy will get flushed down the nursery toilet and cause a flood. Two groups will expect to use the same room at the same time. Much of this can be avoided by having an accessible master calendar available to all the leaders of the congregations. This can be on a public computer or a big paper calendar on a handy wall. Each congregation needs to update it far in advance with their usual room needs, so that other meetings being scheduled don't run into the problem of, "No, that's always our choir rehearsal time in that room!"

Certain areas in the building tend to cause conflict. In the nursery, it's caused by things like messiness or using of materials such as disposable diapers. In the kitchen, it may be messes left uncleaned, refrigerator space taken and again, materials shared. Until the groups get to know each other, especially where there are language barriers, there may be distrust. In one local congregation that shared a building, word began to spread, because one of the women said, "Those people are stealing our dish towels!" Of course, it turned out that another woman in the congregation had taken a large number home to launder. Be very aware if you hear somebody say the words, "Those people..."- that's a powerful red flag that something is going wrong. Talking constantly with members and church committees who deal with these crossover areas will go a long way to make sure communications are happening. Stay plugged in, so issues do not fester. Pastor and staff of the host church have a special role in making sure communication lines stay open. Pastors of the shared churches need to meet regularly to talk out challenges.

D) Keep the Focus Out 50 Years- The Next Generations

I have been told that business planning today thinks of an 18-month horizon as long-term planning. That does not work when rebuilding a congregation in a neighborhood that is being renewed. Our congregation constantly thinks about a 50-year horizon. Since 1988, my work has been focused on preparing an historic congregation for the future. It had been the center of a revival for three generations; when I came, the third generation was dying off. I recognized after the first few years that the congregation needed to discover what God was going to be doing in our neighborhood and city in the next century, and prepare for it. Our educational programs all stem from that vision.

In coming alongside an immigrant congregation, the key questions are how that immigrant congregation will teach its children and transfer its leadership to their English-speaking descendants. So many dozens of issues of respect, power, decision-making, second-generation versus first-generation faith and many more come to bear as that corner is turned. The key area an existing congregation can be of help is in educating the second generation of the congregation. This may be in partnership in Sunday School and youth programs. It may come in intentionality of opening up English-language resources for those children and teens. It may come in simply helping high-English ability teachers understand how to use Sunday School materials.

All around the globe, particularly in the southern hemisphere, where the church is exploding with first-generation believers, the key question is *how do we transmit Christianity to our children?* When I attended the 2010 Lausanne Congress in Cape Town, South Africa, I had many conversations with African and Latin American pastors who themselves were adult conversions, and were trying to understand what faith acquisition looks like in the second generation.

The greatest mistake in American Church history dealt with exactly this question. When my Puritan ancestors entered New England in the 1600s, they were people who had had profound religious conversions. They came to the new land at great cost for religious freedom, and they immersed themselves in Scripture and worship. Their families had daily Bible study, and Sundays were an entire day centered on worship, prayer and God's Word. However, as the decades unfolded, they came to a horrible realization: their children were not having conversion experiences. For these children, who were raised in families who earnestly sought to follow Jesus, their identity from their earliest years was to trust in Christ. They didn't experience conversions! This was devastating to the Puritans, as their theology said that a true Christian had to be able to point to a conversion experience; now their children were not experiencing that kind of entry to faith.

The Puritan church was in a crisis. This is not what they expected! The result was the "Half-Way Covenant" (1662) where the baptized children of the Puritans were allowed partial church membership, but were not allowed to commune until they could testify to having had a conversion experience. Likewise, their children could be baptized, but if they could not put their finger on one particular conversion experience, they too were not allowed to commune. The outcome: *In two generations, the Christian faith had collapsed in New England.*

Thus, for today's first-generation immigrant Christians, their children's experience of faith may be very different from that of their parents. Being raised in dedicated, vibrant homes, by Christian parents who had amazing conversion stories, their faith growth may look very different from their parents. The theology they learn and internalize may be a very, very different understanding than that which their parents learned in their home country. Because of this, both parents and children will need to talk through about what it means to grow up as a Christian child or teen in America. The people doing that teaching will need to have cultural sensitivity for that culture. Children will have many, many questions about how Christians live out their faith in America, because they probably see a very different culture in their public school and TV. Particularly in this area of transmitting faith to the second generation, partnership with an existing congregation can be very helpful, whatever the nurturing theology of the partner congregation.

Thus, as you build alongside an immigrant congregation, working with them to think through the transitions of the next 25-50 years is one of the most critical tasks you face.

E) Find Ways for the Congregations to Work Together

Sitting in pews, staring at the back of each other's heads doesn't do much to create community. Certainly, bringing partner congregations together to share occasional joint worship services is a wonderful idea, but little is accomplished toward building relationships. Building on that, many opportunities appear:

- Joint youth events
- Joint meals or picnics, with intentional mixing of members
- Clean-up, fix-up, paint-up days of the shared facility
- Bringing members of the immigrant church onto the various key committees of the existing congregation, such as Property Management, Youth, Education, etc.
- Celebrate congregational anniversaries or other special events jointly.
- Use holiday worship services to highlight each partner's national customs, foods, etc.
- Together take on a service project in the neighborhood, one that encourages people of each background to take some leadership and work together. Make sure that leadership is spread around, and work with the leaders to make sure it's a good experience for all. Remember that leadership and degree of organization needed for a task may look very different in a different culture.
- Be aware that a disagreement or discomfort with part of a plan may look very different in another culture. Makes sure to talk things over very, very fully.

The Multi-Ethnic Startup Congregation
In the Book of Revelation, we see God's ultimate plan for the church:

> *9 After this I looked, and behold, a great multitude that no one could number, **from every nation, from all tribes and peoples and languages,** standing before the throne and before the Lamb, clothed in white robes, with palm branches in their hands, 10 and crying out with a loud voice, "Salvation belongs to our God who sits on the throne, and to the Lamb!" 11 And all the angels were standing around the throne and around the elders and the four living creatures, and they fell on their faces before the throne and worshiped God, 12 saying, "Amen! Blessing and glory and wisdom and thanksgiving and honor and power and might be to our God forever and ever! Amen."* (Revelation 7:9-12, ESV)

The Church began with much the same vision:

> *When the day of Pentecost arrived, they were all together in one place. 2 And suddenly there came from heaven a sound like a mighty rushing wind, and it filled the entire house where they were sitting. 3 And divided tongues as of fire appeared to them and rested on each one of them. 4 And they were all filled with the Holy Spirit and began to speak in other tongues as the Spirit gave them utterance.*
>
> *5 Now there were dwelling in Jerusalem Jews, devout men from every nation under heaven. 6 And at this sound the multitude came together, and they were bewildered, because each one was hearing them speak in his own language. 7 And they were amazed and astonished, saying, "Are not all these who are speaking Galileans? 8 And how is it that we hear, each of us in his own native language? 9 Parthians and Medes and Elamites and residents of Mesopotamia, Judea and Cappadocia, Pontus and Asia, 10 Phrygia and Pamphylia, Egypt and the parts of Libya belonging to Cyrene, and visitors from Rome, 11 both Jews and proselytes, Cretans and Arabians—we hear them telling in our own tongues the mighty works of God." (Acts 2:1-11, ESV)*

In a moment, the division that came at the Tower of Babel was healed! The early church continued this vision:

> *13 Now there were in the church at Antioch prophets and teachers, Barnabas, Simeon who was called Niger, Lucius of Cyrene, Manaen a lifelong friend of Herod the tetrarch, and Saul. 2 While they were worshiping the Lord and fasting, the Holy Spirit said, "Set apart for me Barnabas and Saul for the work to which I have called them." 3 Then after fasting and praying they laid their hands on them and sent them off. (Acts 13:1-3,* ESV)

At the beginning of the first missionary journey, we see a very mixed group of folks, many who should have instinctively disliked each other, being brought together for the mission of God by the Holy Spirit. There was Barnabas, a Jewish guy from Israel. Simeon, who has a Jewish name, is also called "black" in Latin. Lucius is from North Africa, with a Roman name. Manaen grew up in the "household" of the hated, powerful, amoral Herod family, pretenders to the throne of David and Idumean in background. Finally, we have Saul, (Paul) the multi-cultural mutt- grew up in Asia Minor, Jewish, a Pharisee by training, and a Roman citizen! Way outside the box, God begins his mission to the world not in Jerusalem, not in Israel, but up in the corner of the Mediterranean, in Antioch, the city named after the hated Antiochus Epiphanes who set off the Maccabean revolt by sacrificing a pig in the Jerusalem temple! God has a great sense of humor!

As we see God's desire for the church, we can long for that day in our midst. Were it not for small obstacles such as culture, language and human sin, it would be a snap!

Challenges of the Multicultural Church

The first challenge is language. The multicultural churches, as we are seeing them form in America at this time are primarily made up of 1.5 and second-generation people, joined by the early adopters; people who can all come together and function in a common language, usually English. Most of the "multicultural" churches that are forming today show a great deal of the homogenous unit principle. Even though the members may look very different, often the congregation is made up of young people, with the same economic background, same values, same kind of jobs, and the common experience of being children of immigrants. Some early adopter first-generation immigrants may opt for such a church, just as might those whose families have lived in the US for many generations. Repeated, sequential translation, where one speaker speaks, followed by a translation is very hard on a congregation. It makes all spoken word sections twice as long, and breaks up the continuity of thought in the listeners. It's very hard to sustain interest in a congregation using it weekly.

Real-time simultaneous translation is an option for a multicultural church, like at the UN, where people wear headsets and hear the service translated into their own language. This is costly and difficult; in many cases it's almost impossible for a congregation to come up with a high-level translator for a new immigrant group. This is more difficult than I would have imagined when we started years ago.

The Chinese Lutheran Church in San Francisco, Senior Pastor Hansel Lo, is such a church. On any given Sunday, their worship happens simultaneously in Mandarin, Cantonese, Taiwanese and English. Having the Chinese characters as the basis of the hymns in their hymnal means that they can each read the hymn, and sing it in their own language, all with the same melody; however, the words are all different. They make it work. In the large, highly educated Chinese population of San Francisco, they are able to find able translators.

Many immigrants come here and become proficient in their new language, but to ask them to do real-time translation is beyond the average immigrant's skill level. Years ago, we brought a very gifted Lao man onto our staff. He was the son of a Lao Air Force general, and had been trained as a physician in Laos, China and the Soviet Union. He was a brilliant man, and we thought that we would be able to add real-time Lao translation to our worship service. As educated as he was, we soon realized that he simply did not yet have the English skills to make that service possible, and his outreach would have to go a different direction. The first challenge of the multicultural church is language.

The second challenge is the development of visibly egalitarian leadership. One of the key characteristics of the successful multicultural start-up church is to create the church from the beginning with a multicultural leadership team. Elders and staff need to create a power structure that clearly acts out the congregation's commitment to being multicultural. Only when the worship highlights the music, the languages, the styles, and the faces of every group is the statement publicly being made, power here is being shared.

Dr. Jin Kim is the pastor and developer of Church of All Nations in Minneapolis. A church plant of a Korean Presbyterian church, their website tells of their beginnings:

> In January of 2004, a group of mostly 1.5 and 2nd generation Christians of a Korean immigrant church in Minneapolis was blessed by our "mother church" to launch a multicultural community called Church of All Nations. No one knew if 100 mostly young Korean-Americans could actually become a Church of All Nations; many thought the name was a bit premature, if not presumptuous.

> Our central mission is to do the ministry of reconciliation, and it is happening in all kinds of wonderful ways here. For instance, in January of 2006 we moved from our "mother church" to a declining white PCUSA congregation that had plenty of space. We rented for a few months, but then Shiloh Bethany (Grace) Presbyterian Church asked if they might merge with us. At the end of July, they had a congregational dissolution after being founded

in 1884, and all of their members became members of Church of All Nations, handing us the keys and the title to the building. Incidentally, 1884 is the year that PCUSA missionaries first arrived on the shores of Korea. We came full circle, historically speaking. Not one Shiloh Bethany member left after the merger – praise God! One of the key reasons for this union was the growing recognition of the need to be a new kind of church for an increasingly multicultural population in Columbia Heights and the entire Twin Cities area. Church of All Nations fits that need very well.[17]

Pastor Kim confronts the issue of cultural misunderstandings headlong. He says of his worship service, "Just about every week we remind people that when you come to Church of All Nations, on any given Sunday, someone is probably going to offend you. Don't come to church because it's safe and easy. Work it through, and learn to understand how the offense happened. That's how we grow."

Transforming an Existing Mono-cultural Congregation Into a Multicultural Church

The most difficult challenge in the journey toward a multicultural congregation is changing an existing congregation, with a set power structure, history and culture to be multicultural. Our city is littered thigh-deep with congregations that have tried this and failed miserably. Why have they failed?

Unlike an intentionally planted multicultural church which has a multicultural central power core, an existing church has a culture, an identity, a shared story, perhaps an ethnic identity, probably a certain socio-economic level, a visible power structure based on its Constitution and Bylaws, as well as an invisible power structure of true elders whose attitudes, values and opinions actually guide the congregation. Again using the illustration of you joining the Korean church, you can see all the hurdles it takes for an outsider of a different culture to break into an existing church of a different language or culture. For that person who is visibly of a different ethnicity, there is a vivid separation. Just in joining an existing monocultural congregation of a different background, there is a huge learning curve, beginning with language, culture, history, the names of other members, foods appropriate to bring to a potluck, and much more.   This is why each congregation needs to realize that *they* have a culture, and if they want to be welcoming to even early-adopter immigrants, they will have to learn to do an exceptional job of teaching, welcoming and incorporating.

Just as in partnering with an immigrant congregation depends on intentionally learning the other church's culture, when a congregation receives a member of some immigrant group, it is very important for the congregation to learn about that person's culture. If a congregation is going to try to incorporate people of many cultures, it will have to work specifically and intentionally to welcome publicly and teach about each group.   Highlighting the group's information in worship services, bulletin boards, newsletter articles and such will help the congregation to appreciate the rich cultural heritage and identity of their new members. Music, art or other aspects of that culture can be highlighted in worship or in the celebration of holidays.   Make sure to talk this over with the members of the group, so they feel honored and not displayed as trophies. What you think is interesting or notable about the group may not be the things that the group itself is most proud of.   Talk.

A host congregation needs to figure out their own congregational culture and teach these unwritten rules and norms to the new members. Stop and think about the values and norms of your congregation.   To come to the realization that people of other cultures have perfectly acceptable but differing ways of dealing with time, authority, ownership, priorities, decision making, the importance of money, how the family functions, and a million other things - to realize this is to begin to realize that "we" have a culture, too.

"Our way" is not simply the "normal" way.   It's not even our parents' way.   It's our congregation's culture's way in this time and place.   As we learn this, and learn the cultures of our ministry partners, then and only then can we begin to grow together.   Culture is a snapshot in time of many values.   In five years it may be different, even for the same people.   If we were to travel back in time to visit our own congregation fifty years ago, we might find the worship style, dress, theology and gender roles very uncomfortable!

Yet, at whatever time, if people of differing cultures are to grow together into the Body of Christ, and attain the level of *intimacy*, then a great deal of learning and talking needs to be done to reach that point where the Body of Christ begins to function as the Body of Christ. Will we settle for less?

Chapter Eight:
Models for Church Partnership

As we start talking about partnering with immigrant congregations, the dickens is in the details. When we start talking about structure, we're talking about the good gift of God's law. Somebody said that good fences make for good neighbors. We really don't need fences in the church, but if we think through structural lines of relationships, those relationships can be kept much healthier than if we don't understand what kind of relationship we're trying to build.

Dr. David Ripley, missiologist and one of the founders of the Ethnic America Network, lists ten models he has observed for ways in which congregations can partner in order to create immigrant churches. I use these with his permission, with great admiration and respect. I have added a few notes.[iii] Dr. Ripley reminded me, as he reviewed this section, that a spiritual, Christ-centered relationship between all parties is more important than the model chosen. As we work with idealistic, often first-generation immigrant Christians, living out the "Jesus life" is central to their well-being as believers, and to ours. In living with these believers, who are experiencing first century, first-generation faith, it challenges our example, attitudes, humility and above all, ability to love in Jesus.

As you read this chapter, note the relationships between the circles in the graphics.

1) Host Church Model

1) Host Church Model

This can be simply a rental relationship between the host church and the immigrant group(s).

An existing congregation simply shares their building with another congregation. There may or may not be rent charged. Some of the rent could even be banked so that a baby congregation could take those funds with them when they buy their own building. We have found that sometimes a written lease can be helpful, but over time we have actually become less formal in that area; in most cultures, a handshake is adequate. That might not be the best idea for each situation. Even so, it's good to discuss as many issues as possible- who is responsible for locking the building when both groups are there; worship times, storage and so on. This model is based simply on sharing a particular space.

2) Department Church Model

2) Department Church Model

The ethnic group is organized as a church department expressed as an adult community or Sunday School class.

Particularly in a larger congregation that is successful in outreach to immigrants, one way to relate is simply to think of the ministry to that group as a department of the congregation. This gives them all the structural support of a congregation- budget lines, Sunday School in English for their children, shared use of a building, staff and programing. However, it does keep the existing congregation very much in control, and the immigrants may always feel isolated or as second-class members, due to their isolation. If the congregation was particularly good at welcoming the group and kept them visible and feeling a respected part of the larger congregation, this can work.

3) Multi-Congregational Model

3) Multi-Congregational Model

Ethnic groups form different congregations where everyone is a member of the same church

Much like number two, this approach is different in that immigrant groups are set up to be their own congregation, but everyone is a member of the same church. This model is about a shared building, shared costs, with a degree of independence. The groups may or may not move toward some sort of unification in the second generation.

4) Outreach Model

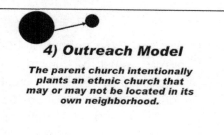

4) Outreach Model

The parent church intentionally plants an ethnic church that may or may not be located in its own neighborhood.

An existing congregation intentionally plants an immigrant congregation. It might be in a shared building, or in an independent satellite site that would be strategically sited to reach a particular population. As we have said before, the right "touch" is important, that the existing congregation relates to its offspring with mutual trust and respect, not paternalism.

5) Partnership Model

5) Partnership Model

Churches with different ethnic backgrounds come together to plant another ethnic or multi-ethnic church.

This is a fascinating model in that it would bring existing churches of various backgrounds together to work in harmony to plant another congregation. Although there would be great challenges, the gains in mutual understanding and learning to work together across cultural boundaries would be a tremendous learning experience!

6) Adoption Model

6) Adoption Model

A church adopts an existing ethnic fellowship to help encourage and strengthen that ministry.

This has great potential for help IF the larger church minds its manners. A large church has resources and ways of supporting a baby congregation that could be quite useful. Again, if the larger church can be supportive while fostering independence, like a parent to a child, it can work well. Paternalistic attitudes on behalf of the adopting church, or creating financial dependence will destroy the adopted church in the long run.

7) Assimilation Model

7) Assimilation Model

All ethnic believers are absorbed into the host church and adjust to its programs and styles.

As we have talked about it before, most of the members who join an existing congregation of a different language will be that small group who are early adopters. I would not expect that most existing congregations could hope that this would be a way for them to grow. Yet, in the Roman Catholic churches, this is a widely seen pattern. Because congregations are organized to serve a given area, Roman Catholics in that area are expected to join that parish's church. Those congregations struggle with incorporating these new folks, inevitably adopting some version of one of these models, however, when the congregation is small, there simply is no other option. The congregation moves forward not because of commonalities but because of formal structure. Another example of this that did work was an existing congregation in our area. An entire congregation of Liberians all came together with their pastor and asked to join the existing congregation, if their pastor could be hired by the established church. The congregations merged, and the group was accepted into the congregation's power structure.

8) Multi-Church Model

8) Multi-Church Model

Several autonomous fellowships use the same church building where they are involved in their own governance.

Something like models two and three, the difference here is that there is one building, but several independent congregations, each with their own governance, budgets, worship, structures, etc. This structure could work very well if a denomination would take an unused building and use it as a conveyor-belt ethnic church planting strategy.

9) Multi-Ethnic Model

8) Multi-Church Model

Several autonomous fellowships use the same church building where they are involved in their own governance.

This is something like number seven, but there are large enough groups of people of a given people group that they have distinct identity within the congregation. Perhaps there would be some special events, language-specific meetings that would allow these members to have a sense of belonging to a greater church while still having a group where they could all share the same culture.

10) Blended Model

10) Blended Model

One church may be involved in more than one model as it works out its ethnic church planting activities.

This model recognizes that a given congregation could be involved via more than one of these models simultaneously. What works, works. Relationships with immigrant congregations need to be worked out as dynamic, flexible and supportive. The existing congregation must enter these relationships with humility, a teachable spirit and an expectation that there will be challenges and bumps all along the road. The outcome or end may or may not be glorious, but what is learned and what is experienced along the way will not only be a remarkable experience, it will also be a tremendous time of learning. With each congregation we have partnered, we have learned a bit more about the process, our expectations and what not to do. Even so, these partnerships have been among the greatest experiences of my 40 years of ministry.

We thus have many models of how to do shared ministry. The next key is how to begin. The next chapter will give you some concrete ideas on how you as a congregation or you as an individual can get started.

Chapter Nine: How to Get Started:
God's Call to Cross Boundaries

Most of the new people coming here as a part of God's diaspora are not Christians; they have never begun to hear the gospel. Most have no idea who Jesus Christ is. The church today faces this challenge: Will we reach out in the name of Jesus? Will we reach out to the new immigrants in our midst?

The future of America and the future of the American church will be decided by what we do in this generation. What lies ahead could be a "balkanized" America, America torn apart like the Balkans, like Yugoslavia, where there are many nationalities and very hardened cultural walls. Today, we're still breaking through our own walls, like those between Anglos and African-Americans or Anglos and Native-Americans. Those walls have become very hardened in some places, and very difficult boundaries to break through into relationships.

What will happen to the new groups who come into the United States; will we learn to cross over the boundaries between us? Today in the US, we easily cross old boundaries between Norwegian and Swede, or Norwegian and Irish, or German and Greek. A hundred years ago, these were difficult boundaries to cross because of religious, language, cultural and historical barriers. We found ways to make those boundaries permeable. It will be decided in our generation, primarily by the work of the church, whether we will have hard boundaries or permeable boundaries with our new immigrant groups. The only unifying factor we have is the person of Jesus Christ. The next decade will decide the future of America.

The goal of Mission*Shift* is that in this generation, every congregation in America will have its own simple cross-cultural ministry. Just like it has a Sunday School or a women's group or a property committee, we encourage each church to create, in whatever form works for them, their own means of reaching out to some ethnic-specific group, unreached in your community.

This ministry may change as each group is reached, or as the ethnic makeup of a given area changes over time. As we talk about building ministries, we need to think about ministries of congregations and ministries of individuals, just regular church members in their day-to-day lives. Those two areas are the focus of this chapter.

First, we want these new neighbors to come to know Jesus Christ.

That's the center of what we do. This desire is not mean, it is not judgmental, it is not triumphalistic; we believe Jesus is the greatest gift we have and the center of God's will for each individual. We believe that coming to know Jesus Christ is the only thing that can unify us, because he unifies us.

This kind of ministry is contingent on the acculturation curves we discussed in Chapter Two. These can help us to understand the differing forms of outreach we need to use at given times and places as people come, as they enter, and as they become more acculturated. We learned how people at the beginning of their acculturation will be reached by those helping them with their needs and building relationships. Any sort of church or Bible study with this beginning group will of course need to be in their heart language. We can help in many ways for that to happen.

Ministry-Specific or *Group*-Specific

As we begin to build these ministries to immigrants, it may develop to be either *ministry*-specific or *group*-specific. In other words, the ministry will stay the same, but the group you minister to changes, or, you continue with the same people group and change your ministry to fit their changing needs. You might create a ministry such as ESL, English as a Second Language, (we may wish to call it ELL, English Language Learners, because this may not be their second language. It may be their fourth or fifth!) ESL is a great ministry for churches to start. There are few costs, no expensive equipment, and even a teacher with minimal training can be very effective. With hordes of Baby Boomers approaching retirement, and millions of immigrants, this is a very attractive approach. There are even materials available that weave Bible stories into the lessons, to begin to create some understanding of Christianity's message. We can bring this critical skill, share the Bible message and build relationships all at the same time! This can be offered almost anywhere. In the past decade the location and number of immigrants has so changed that almost any church in any community will find themselves in the midst of those they can reach. Classes could continue on toward job-readiness or citizenship.

You will probably begin these ministries with a predominance of a particular ethnic population. That group may pass through and in five years we will find ourselves working with a different ethnic community. Your ministry may remain much the same, in the same place, with the same volunteers, but you may need to culturally tweak it a bit, because the predominant group may change. In our church neighborhood, we have had eleven distinct waves of ethnic groups in our neighborhood over the past 30 years, but for the last decade, due to extensive improvement in the housing stock and the formation of an urban "ethnoburb," we have seen a long-term presence of Latinos and Somalis. In your area, as in all areas, what you can count on is change. What you build today will have to change as your area changes.

You might create a ministry to a given group, and as time passes your ministry changes as you continue to specialize in work with that particular culture. Perhaps you would begin with a welcoming ministry, with classes on how to buy groceries, how to travel by mass transit, how to vacuum a floor, use a stove, how to dress for winter, walk on ice, or the purposes of all those strange porcelain things in the bathroom. For people raised in hot climates, who spent a generation or two in a primitive refugee camp, whose food

Sidebar: Legal Dangers

When working with populations of undocumented immigrants, major precautions must be taken when doing holistic ministry. It is very easy to commit a Federal felony while simply doing common sense care and support!

These laws and policies are constantly changing, as are state laws and policies of enforcement. Because of this, if working with a group, you should be in touch with local representatives of Homeland Security and/or a local immigration attorney.

In the past, ministries have gotten in trouble by providing services to undocumented immigrants such as arranging employment, providing sheltering or even providing transportation to ESL/ELL classes. This is not an exhaustive list, and ministries must protect themselves and their workers by clarifying with Homeland Security what has been provided for them, these will all be critical new skills. These are things that we take for granted, but are part of that immensely difficult beginning period in a new culture. Remember, these will all need to be taught with an interpreter, or with improvised sign language. Even so, they will never forget that you came alongside them in their hour of need.

Realize too that those at this point of the steep learning curve, your immigrants may be dealing with a great deal of depression and/or post-traumatic stress disorder. They are at a time where they probably will not have the ego strength to reciprocate in friendship or do more than survive. You may not get many emotional "strokes," and your new friends may seem to be ungrateful "takers." That is because of their intense need to turn inward, re-establish their identity and just deal with the critical tasks of life. A person drowning has little else on their mind but survival in that moment. A relationship will take time.

As you build relationships, you may find that you wish to continue your work with this group. They will need to find English classes and other work-readiness skills. They will need to learn to communicate with their children's schools. Their children may need after-school tutoring. They will need to learn about American hospitals, dental care, immunizations and normal relationships with a physician or clinic. All of these will be new and perhaps alarming for them. As time goes on, they will learn more and more. They will get some sort of more-permanent job. They will buy a car and need to learn to care for it. They will move to better neighborhoods, better housing, and in a few years even purchase a home, much to their delight. They will deal with social service agencies, governmental units, immigration issues, and avoiding those who prey financially on immigrants. Some will build businesses, and bringing retired entrepreneur-mentors into their lives could be a great ministry! Through all these things, you can come alongside, listen, befriend, mentor, and share both your world and Lord. You will need to set up boundaries, such as not loaning money, no romantic involvements, etc. In most cultures, it is best to have men work with men and women work with women.

Frustrating and Rewarding

This sort of *group*-specific ministry can be very rewarding, but you have to be ready for a long-term commitment, frustration, huge challenges and the very real probability that they will move far away, due to family or job. Your immigrants will probably move many times. Most likely, the churches in the new neighborhood will be clueless and have no vision or desire to take over their care, so you will continue to do ministry, even as distance increases. Your ministry will change as they move along the acculturation curve.

If they do move far away, is all your work in vain? Have you invested all that work and your church hasn't gained any members? It's not about us. It's about them. It's about the Gospel. Paul tells us, *So neither he who plants nor he who waters in anything, but only God who gives the growth. He who plants and he who waters are one, and each will receive his wages according to his labor. For we are God's fellow workers. (1 Corinthians 3:7-8)* We have to change our idea of results. We have to trust the work of the Holy Spirit. Our outcome is measured in eternity. This is not naive, idealistic thinking; this is the very heart of the Gospel.

Think Long-Term, not the Latest Shiny Object!

A long-term commitment to a group or even a family can be extremely effective in the long-term. Fifty years from now, that family will still remember your love. They and their family will have come to know about Jesus, and hopefully, know Jesus. You will probably not plant a megachurch, but your impact on that small group will be immeasurable. Remember, you don't hit oil by digging a thousand holes one foot deep. This kind of ministry is more about the journey than the destination. It's about walking alongside immigrants on their journey. The ultimate goal is to find their place in the Body of Christ, but that journey will be a lot more like walking through a brushy forest, full of obstacles, rather than walking across an empty football field. You will take many turns and detours, that's the norm, but Jesus will bring you through.

These ministries will often have a lifespan of three to five years. For immigrants, their world is constantly changing. If a ministry finishes its work in that span, that is perfectly normal. You accomplished what you needed to accomplish at that time and place. Perhaps it will morph into something else; perhaps there will be a new group or a new need that appears. We mustn't fear change, nor measure our success in terms of stability. Work with immigrants revels in the constant chaos. Control is not possible, because of all the challenges of culture, old traumas, growing children, job instability, poverty and just general chaos. If you need control and order, you will not find it in immigrant ministry, or any other kind of ministry for that matter. Original sin gives us a very insecure base for all we do. We pray, work, hope, laugh, fail, celebrate little victories, and know that God is at work constantly. This is the central challenge for the global church in the 21ˢᵗ Century. We are no longer dealing with the stable Christendom of the 1950s. God is up to something remarkable. Climb in and hang on!

Because of the intensity of this work, and the need for faithful focus, many of the churches who are doing the best with immigrants are small- to medium-sized congregations. They don't need vast resources, they need vision and commitment. A few megachurches get it, and with a special core of people who feel called to a certain ministry, they can accomplish great things. However, I find that most megachurches have a bad case of the "shiny object syndrome." Staff are driven to produce results, find the next exciting thing, keep the church attractive to religious consumers who want to have that next cool experience. Last year it was a mission trip to the Amazon. This year it's solving world hunger.

No.

Simple believers, with a heart for Jesus and neighbor will change this world. It will take an investment of heart and mind, but can be accomplished in a few hours per week. Plan your ministry so you don't need to be superhuman to make it happen. Draw some friends in. Think in terms of less than five hours per week of involvement. Keep it simple. You don't need to start with a budget or by creating a 501c3 organization. Our Mission*Shift* Institute functioned for almost 15 years without a 501c3, bylaws or formal structure. It wasn't needed yet. Our congregation's treasurer simply cut the checks, and funds ran through a special budget line. That was adequate, yet it had proper oversight. Any big donations were eligible for tax deductions because of our congregation's credentials. Keep it simple, build what you need, keep it flexible. Add structure only as needed, and be willing to follow the Spirit and dismantle precious structure when the times change. Think of ministry more in terms of living in tents rather than in houses.

One of the bottom-line realities of glocal, diaspora ministry is that you need to think in terms of a five-year commitment. The ministry may have run its course a bit before that, but we cannot enter this kind of ministry thinking in the terms of doing the latest, trendy thing. It's not six weeks of studying this new popular book, or an exciting eight-week course taught by the newest, slickest video Bible teacher. It's going to take time. It's going to have some frustration involved. It's not going to be easy, and probably at some point will appear to be impossible. But God will break through. Most importantly, it's going to change you from a religious consumer in the pew to what God wants you to be: a front-line, cross-cultural missionary! "Out there" is now right here.

The definition of success will be in the relationships and the outcomes in individual lives over long-term, and in eternity. Your church can be a tool of the Holy Spirit along the way, as these people pass through.

What Can You Do as an Individual?

Most of the immigrants who have come to our congregation have come there because someone in the congregation befriended them. One of our members is a friendly senior citizen who has a particular gift in meeting people. He strikes up conversations with the immigrant who is the checkout guy at Home Depot. After meeting the guy, he makes note of his name. When he stops by the store a few weeks later, he talks to him a bit more. He works to build a relationship. He's got a great shop in his garage, where he teaches immigrants simple car repairs and the use of tools. He likes outdoor activities, and invites this guy and a friend to an afternoon outing. Realize that many immigrants would love to have an American friend. It's as simple as that.

One of our seniors spent her life as a missionary in the tribal region of Pakistan. She is fluent in Urdu, and has a great heart for Muslim people. This obviously gives her some amazing tools for ministry, however, the people that she brings to church are simply neighbors in the same apartment building. They don't necessarily speak Urdu. They barely speak English. But they are eager to have a real friend.

A key connection in our area is the hunger of Muslim women to have an "American" friend. They are eager to learn how our women think, how they cook, how they relate to their husbands, how they raise their children and how they live in such freedom in America. On the television, they see many bad role models, and they worry tremendously about their children. Don't we all? When they learn that not all the Americans they see on TV are Christians, and that there are Americans who share their exact concerns, they are very, very eager to form bonds. Calvary Lutheran Church in Golden Valley, MN, a first-ring suburb here, has built a quilting ministry, where Somali women and church members come together to quilt, to talk, and to build relationships. For a group with a culture as distant as theirs is from ours, this is a tremendous ministry. These women are building trust, heart-to-heart, face-to-face and faith-to-faith.

Distances of Culture

When Billy Graham called together the first Lausanne Congress on World Evangelization in 1974, this marked many firsts. It was the beginning of a new cooperation between mission agencies in tracking "unreached people groups" and coordinating resources toward them. It marked the beginning of using computers to create these databases. It also marked the "baptizing" of sociology and anthropology to transmit Christianity more effectively and culturally neutral.

A key paper shared at that event was "The New Macedonia – A Revolutionary New Era in Mission Begins," by Ralph D. Winter.[18] It has been widely re-printed, such as in the *Mission Perspectives* course book, and is available online. It is worth a few minutes to read. In that seminal essay, Winter outlined the distinction between cultures that are closer to one's own, versus cultures that are very different. He uses the terms E-1, E-2, and E-3 to arbitrarily show levels of distance between cultures. For example, when Americans try to communicate with Mexican people, these cultures are not very distant. Winter would call that distance E-1. They find that they both have some understanding of the basics of Christianity. They both come with a common shared European history and philosophy, albeit separated by a few hundred years of individual history. They have languages that share about 70 percent of vocabulary. Because of a shared border and tourism, both cultures have interacted extensively. Even so, the languages are different enough to be a barrier. A history of antagonism and racism can divide members of the two groups. There are many shared values, but also great differences. Even so, the commonality makes learning each other's culture a bit easier, an E-1 relationship.

Contrasting this with Somalis, we see a great difference. Their culture would be categorized a much more distant E-3. Before their refugee ordeal began, a high percentage of Somalis were wandering pastoralists, much like Sarah and Abraham. They did not have a written language until the 1970s. Their language shares almost no words with English. Its structure and thought patterns are different. They are a clan-based society with a long history of inter-clan violence. Most had practiced an animistic form of Islam, but have been greatly influenced by radical Saudi-financed Wahhabi missionaries in the Kenyan camps. Some have been taught to be very distrustful of Christians and the church. The expectations of the cultural roles of women and men are radically different from American values. This list could go on for several pages. Winter would term this greater cultural distance as E-3.

The reason I mention this is that as an individual or congregation enters into cross-cultural immigrant ministry, glocal ministry, it is critical to do your homework. The more distant a group's culture, the more learning it will take. We can enter this work with no presuppositions that any way that we think the world works is the same for a person of another culture. In fact, for every "fact" that you know about how the world works, someone, somewhere, of another culture understands it the opposite. The more distant the culture, the more learning and less presupposing we can do.

As I said in Chapters Five and Six on planning and training, we have many tools available to give us background to learn about our neighbors. Learning about their path to our country, the situation there that pushed them to leave, their worldview, culture and values all will help us to more quickly build a relationship. Learning some phrases in their language shows respect and opens doors. Learning to be a listener, learning to give people of other cultures the gift of our time, learning their stories, learning about their families, and more are the paths to relationship.

In most of the world, time is not seen as such a scarce commodity. Patty Lane tells a story of her friendship with an Egyptian Christian woman:

> "When I was a seminary student, I had a good friend from Egypt. She was a seminary student as well, and in between work, study, church and classes, we tried to spend time together. One day at her apartment, she made a startling announcement to me. She said quite definitively, "You know Americans are just too busy to be Christians." As you can imagine, I was surprised to hear her say that, so I asked her to explain what she meant. She replied, "Americans, even those who call themselves Christians, are always having to do something or go somewhere. They say they care about you, but they never stop by just to visit. When they call you, it is just for a few minutes, and is usually because they

need to get some information from you, and not to see how you are. They talk about serving God and loving people, but I don't see how they can when they are so busy and have so much to do. Do they think God wants them to live like that? I don't think they care what God wants. They have their schedules, and that is their god. How can a real Christian survive here?"[19]

In my relationships with East Africans, I have learned that when I ask, "How are you?" most will now answer the standard American, "Good." However, if I am to enter their culture, I need to follow up with more questions. "How is your family?" "How is your wife?" "How are your children doing in school?" "How is your work going?" Several times, I've seen a reaction of a double-take as I ask the second question, inevitably followed by a smile. That is the East African norm. In approaching them in their cultural way, and actually showing care, trusting friendships also build quickly. Ethiopians shake hands by bowing, and as a sign of respect, they reach with their left hand, and support their right elbow. I started doing this, and learned more when one of their leaders told me that I would make younger people feel uncomfortable if I did the "elbow thing" when shaking hands with them. There is so much to learn!

The Treasure Hunt Begins: Go do Some Research!

Yet, learning is the key way in which we will welcome these new friends to know our friend, Jesus. More and more books and resources on other cultures are becoming available constantly, but you can quickly do your own research with the scads of information available online. (Many more places to search are listed back in Chapter Three.) Another tool that is of great use is the good old paper-based Encyclopaedia Britannica. Even though they have quit publishing the paper version, find a late set, or stop by your public library. I own one set for home and one for the office! There is no comparable resource that goes into the depth of the Macropaedia articles on the history of each country, region and religion. I am saddened that this resource is not still being printed. It is of a depth far beyond anything available yet online. Once you have done your first introductory research online, in a couple hours in the library with the Britannica you can get a depth of information unparalleled.

Wikipedia, for all its inaccuracies created by its numerous amateur writers, is still an excellent starting point for your first foray in learning about a people group. Search for other websites that tell the history of your group, share its culture, its myths, its history, its foods, its religious understandings. See if you can find anyone from that culture critiquing Christianity, which may give you some clues as to what gets in the way of the Gospel for them. Up to date information on their homeland can be found online at the CIA's World Fact Book. As you do your research, keep copying the URL addresses and make notes as to what you found there. The Internet is so immense that it's hard to find a particular resource a second time! Another danger is that websites are constantly being updated, so URLs may be abandoned quickly- keep a good description. These technologies are so new that it's hard to anticipate how we will find archived materials from a few years past. If you find a particularly useful site, you may even wish to take a screen shot or print those pages. Ah, technology!

Sharing a Building

Sharing a church can be a challenge; it takes a great deal of communication in order to avoid and settle conflict. Our congregation has now shared our building with six congregations and several smaller ministries. Each has been a different kind of relationship, according to the other congregation's wants and needs. Some have wanted us to take a very active role in mentoring them. Some have simply wanted to use space and run their program. Some have just used office or education space. We have found that we need to keep careful track of keys, including charging a re-keying fee in case the loaned keys are not returned at the end of their time of sharing the building. Keeping the pastors and leaders of the various aspects of the congregations talking to one another is the key. Cultural differences will have to be addressed from time to time as misunderstandings and misattributions happen. Chapter Six had several ideas on how to bring two congregations together.

The Mission*Shift* DVD Video Series

Another tool to begin to wake up your congregation, adult Sunday School, cell group or youth group is the Mission*Shift* DVD series. This six-session video series does a great job to introduce this entire topic and covers, in an abridged version, many of the topics of this book. Churches, non-profits, universities and seminaries all over the U.S. are using it. It is available on our Mission*Shift* website: www.MissionShift.org

The DVDs also have a built-in free curriculum that you can edit as you wish. It has Bible studies, discussion questions, even games and other ideas on how to enhance the material.

Knees and Sneeze

One of the most amazing simple experiences of evangelism our congregation has experienced is something we called "Knees and Sneeze." After studying the Gospel of John, we noticed that after people encountered Jesus, they just blurted out, "bore witness" and told about Jesus. That's the power of the Gospel! John tells the story, that this truth about Jesus infects the hearers, like cold causes us to sneeze and pass the cold on. One summer, I asked the congregation to make a commitment. I asked them to pray each morning, "Lord, please send me one person today whom you have prepared to hear the Gospel, and tell me what I need to say. In Jesus' Name, Amen." The entire congregation signed a pledge with those words. Then things started happening.

Later that morning, my introverted, shy wife prayed that prayer, and then stopped by the grocery store to pick something up on the way home. As she approached the cash register, the young Asian man running the register looked at her, and said, "Did you go to church this morning? You need to pray with me." Shocked, she did.

A couple days later one of our Council members prayed that and went to work. She added, "And please make it very obvious who I'm supposed to talk to." A little while after she got to work, her office-mate came in, loudly dropped her books on her desk, and said, "I wish somebody would please tell me my purpose." Our member, just to be sure, said, "You mean the purpose of your job?" "No," her friend answered, "The purpose of my life."

Bingo.

As we are open, as we open our eyes, our hearts and our lips, our God can do amazing things. We stand at one of the most important crossroads of human history. The future of the American church, the global church, and the future of America are at stake.

Now is the time to start.

Endnotes:

1.Estimates regarding the urbanization of the globe vary, depending on what is considered a city, anywhere from 50,000 to one million. Some countries have very uncertain population statistics. Suffice it to say that humanity is rapidly moving to cities.

2. Thomas L Friedman, *The World is Flat: A Brief History of the Twenty-First Century*, (New York: MacMillan - Farrar, Straus and Giroux, 2005)

3. During the peacetime draft, c. 1951-71, a normal draft deferment allowed college students to avoid conscription until they graduated, if they remained full-time students with at least a 3.00 grade point average. However, the divinity deferment continued through college and seminary, and upon graduation there was no requirement to serve in the army. This made it the most desirable deferment, as the student would never have to face being drafted. When the draft ended, mainline seminary enrollments plummeted.

9. Website: http://static1.businessinsider.com/image/4e450c056bb3f7b743000049/chart.jpg

10. For the past century this has been the rule, however today with core-city neighborhoods being gentrified, with governmental policies changing to spread low-income housing more broadly in metro areas, and with the huge number of immigrants entering, today immigrants will enter anywhere they can find a job. Anywhere can and will be a gateway neighborhood today.

11. Walter Rauschenbusch, *A Theology for the Social Gospel*

(New York: The MacMillan Company, 1918)

12. Conversation, Dr. Roy Harrisville, Jr., Luther Seminary at St. Paul, Minnesota, c. 1998

ii Sittler, Joseph, Lecture at the ALC Equipping the Saints event at St. Olaf College, Northfield, MN, June, 1981.

13. Matthew 9:13 - at the call of Matthew and Matthew 12:7, at the culmination of a teaching about "something greater than the temple is here," Jesus quotes this verse, signifying that now that the Temple is destroyed, faith in Jesus is the continuation of the OT *chesed* relationship, not the Pharisees' rules.

14. Walther Zimmerli, *"chesed,"* in *Theological Dictionary of the New Testament,* ed.G.Kittel and G. Friedrich, trans. And ed. Geoffrey W. Bromiley, (Grand Rapids: Wm. B. Eerdmans Publishing, 1974) IX:381-387

15. Exo. 22: 22-25, Deut 10:18, Deut 24:17, Isa 10:1-2,

16. Patty Lane, *A Beginner's Guide to Crossing Cultures,* (Downers Grove: InterVarsity Press, 2002)

17. Wells, Roland. Paper: A Qualitative Study on Perception of Life-Change of Students of the School of Urban Ministry. Submitted for D Min project at Luther Seminary, January, 2009

18. https://joshuaproject.net/assets/media/articles/the-highest-priority.pdf

19. http://www.npr.org/templates/story/story.php?storyId=5391395

20. Lane, *A Beginner's Guide to Crossing Cultures.*

21. Salomón, Esaúl and Melissa. *Harvest Waiting: Reaching Out to the Mexicans.* (St. Louis: Concordia Publishing House,

1995)

22. http://www.cando.org/our-history/   2/25/14

[iii] Dr David L Ripley contact information:

SIM USA (retired…formerly Director of the Ethnic Ministries Department, Billy Graham Center at Wheaton College)
1102 Ghana St, Sebring, FL   33875
dgripley@yahoo.com 863-382-2553 (H) 630-696-2643 (C)

23. http://www.etnopedia.info/?p=769
Winter would go on to create the US Center for World Mission in Pasadena, California and author many key resources for the expansion of the Kingdom.

24. Lane, Patty. *A Beginner's Guide to Crossing Cultures,* p. 101-102.

Printed in Great Britain
by Amazon

27263898R00090